This volume is dedicated to the youth of the working class

Index

	Page
The Assassination of Leon Trotsky	1
Trotsky Explains the Dialectic	23
Hegel's Doctrine of Essence	31
Engels on the Identity of Thought and Being	43
Philosophical Materialism	48
Workers Control and the State.	54
The Logic of Capital	60
The Dialectical 'Cell' of Nature and Capitalism - G. Healy	68
The Soviet Thermidor	76
Book Review - Architect or Bee by Mike Cooley	104
Our National Freedom	114
The Moscow Trials	119
Letter to John Gollan - G. Healy	133
The Elements of Dialectics	136
Letters to a Group	148
Marxism and Statistics	156
Hegel's Remarks on the Doctrine of Essence	161
Trade Unions in the Epoch of Imperialist Decay - Leon Trotsky	169

The Assassination of Leon Trotsky

On 21ˢᵗ August 1940 Harrold Robins, the chief guard at Trotsky's fortified house at Coyoacan, Mexico, was standing near to the door to Trotsky's study. He heard a commotion inside and stepped towards the door to investigate, but it opened before he could get there. Trotsky emerged, holding his head, blood pouring down:

"My God, look what they have done to me", he said, and collapsed to the floor.

Robins entered the room and saw the assassin, Jac Monard alias Ramon Mercader, holding an alpine ice axe in one hand and a Spanish *Star* .45 inch calibre automatic pistol in the other. He stepped towards Mercader and struck his head with the heavy Smith and Wesson .45 inch calibre revolver he was holding. Mercader collapsed to the floor and was later arrested and charged with murder. Trotsky died hours later, but said again and again, "Make him talk – make him talk." This was the measure of Trotsky, his first thought was so see how his organisation had been penetrated. The last message he gave us was, "I have every confidence in the future of the Forth International – Go forward!"

How had the assassin got to Trotsky?

It was not that Trotsky did not know the danger he was in, no one knew the nature of the GPU murder machine better than he. They had recently murdered his son and three of his close comrades, and only the previous 24ᵗʰ May a gang of Stalinist murderers had penetrated the outer defence of the compound and unleashed a hail of bullets from sub-machineguns and hurled fire-bombs through the windows. Trotsky threw himself to the floor and survived by pure chance.

So what was the true nature and extent of the threat to Trotsky's life, what defensive measures were in place at the house and how were they penetrated?

Following the raid in May Trotsky took the most stringent security measures, transforming his house into a virtual military installation. A military engineer was engaged, electrically controlled steel gates were installed and guard towers were made bullet proof, all visitors were strictly vetted, and much besides. Should not all this have been meticulously reviewed and analysed to find what went wrong? Above all, why was there no attempt to find out how the Fourth International had been so comprehensively penetrated and who was involved? The man responsible for Trotsky's security, for his very life, was Joseph Hansen, a leading member of the American Socialist Workers Party, but his only involvement seems to have been to select the guards in the United States and send them down to the house. We know that he was present in the house when the crime was committed and that he must have been aware of his responsibilities, but there is no record of him carrying out any kind of investigation and he made no report. How then *did* he respond to this catastrophic blow at the World Revolution? How did he report it to the Fourth International and the working class?

All we have is a self-effacing article in the SWP press intitled *With Trotsky to the End.* The story then, is not about Trotsky, but about Hansen himself, and the picture he paints is totally at odds with the reality. He implies that Trotsky disliked elaborate security measures and under a sub-heading, *Could we Have Prevented It?* which clearly implies that nothing could have been done and no blame can be attached to himself as Trotsky's chief bodyguard, he writes:

"Since September 1937 Trotsky's secretaries tried to institute as system in the household whereby everyone who entered would be searched for concealed weapons. They also attempted to make it an iron rule that Trotsky was never to talk with anyone alone in his study. Trotsky would not endure either of these rules ... Trotsky had dozens upon dozens of friends in Mexico, whom the guards – so far as their vigilance was concerned – placed in the same general category as Jacson (Merceda) before the assault." (Quoted in *How The GPU Murdered Trotsky*, page 221, New Park Publications.)

This stands out in the starkest contrast to the information we have, only some of which we have related above. Here we have a man who is under direct threat from the Stalinist murder machine, who has just escaped with his life in the recent raid, whose son and many of his comrades have been murdered, who has just engaged a military engineer to fortify his house, and Hansen tells us that he was careless about his own security! We shall see below what motivated Hansen to paint such a ludicrously false picture.

The Seeds of Betrayal

The nature and extent of the threat to Trotsky was no mystery. It began to take shape following the death of Lenin and the rise to power of the Stalinist reaction. To consolidate his power Stalin found it necessary to wipe out the whole Bolshevik leadership of the Revolution by any means, most importantly Trotsky himself. His method was lies and slander, false accusation and frame up, imprisonment, torture and assassination. The record appears to us now like a bloody trail from the Kremlin right up to the door of Trotsky's study and inside. Here we shall recount no more that is necessary to show the truth.

The seeds of betrayal of the Revolution were already present in the Bolshevik Party in 1917. Lenin had been absent in exile for years and the theoretical life of the Bolshevik Party had suffered badly. According to the Marxist understanding of historical development the feudal era must necessarily pass into capitalism, and in the fulness of time, due to its own internal logic, capitalism must be transformed into socialism through workers revolution. Those Bolsheviks present in Petrograd concluded, therefore, that since it was a revolution to overthrow feudalism, the present revolution must usher in an era of capitalism, with the possibility of socialism a distant prospect. During the weeks following the February 1917 revolution Bolshevik leaders began to arrive in Petrograd having been released from prison and exile. Among them were two Bolsheviks, Stalin and Kamenev, who managed to get a controlling position on the editorial board of the Bolshevik paper, *Pravda*. The old editors were removed as being too "left" and the new editors adopted a position of support for the Provisional Government and support for the war.

Then, on 4th. April, Lenin arrived in Petrograd and submitted his famous *April Theses* to a meeting of Bolsheviks. (See Lenin Collected Works, Vol. 24, page 21.) Insisting that Marxist theory is not a dogma but a guide to action, be fought fiercely to re-orientate the Party. Fiercely condemning the position taken by Stalin and Kamenev on both the nature of the revolution and the war, he explained in the *First Thesis:*

> "The class conscious proletariat can give its consent to a revolutionary war, which would really justify revolutionary defensism, only on condition: a) that the power pass to the proletariat and poorest sections of the peasants aligned with the proletariat; b) that all annexations be renounced in deed and not in word; c)

that a complete break be effected in actual fact with all capitalist interests."

Clearly Stalin and Kamenev had been supporting a capitalist regime and an imperialist predidatory war! In the *Second Thesis* Lenin explains the nature of the revolution:

> "The specific feature of the present situation in Russia is that the country is passing from the first stage of the revolution – which, owing to the insufficient class-consciousness and organisation of the proletariat, placed power in the hands of the bourgeoisie – to its second stage, which must place power in the hands of the proletariat and the poorest sections of the peasants."

He goes on to explain that while the February revolution had overthrown the tsarist regime, and in this sense was a *bourgeois* revolution to bring in the capitalist era, the capitalists, the bourgeoisie themselves, were not capable of forming a stable regime in their own name, and that it was necessary for the proletariat to impose *its own* regime, the rule of the soviets and the transition to socialism, or all would be lost, tsarism would be restored and a period of reactionary dictatorship would follow. Contrary to the general view of the Marxists, therefore, the bourgeois stage of history would be "skipped over", and feudalism would proceed straight to socialism. But the "old Bolsheviks" as they called themselves, simply could not comprehend this. Days after the publication of the *Theses* they wrote the following in Pravda:

> "As for the general scheme of Comrade Lenin, it seems to us unacceptable in that it starts from the assumption that the bourgeois-democratic revolution is ended, and counts upon an immediate transformation of this revolution into a socialist revolution."

This was the situation when Trotsky arrived at the Finland railway station in Petrograd in May and received a tumultuous welcome. There were representatives from the Central Committee of the Bolshevik Party and from his own organisation, the Inter-District group. This was most significant since Trotsky had finally abandoned his attempts to re-unite the Bolsheviks and Mensheviks and adopted the same internationalist position as Lenin, *revolutionary-defeatism,* to unite the working class across the belligerent countries in a revolutionary struggle to use the war to hasten the downfall of capitalism. At the same time he had arrived at the same position as Lenin on the nature of the Revolution through his own development of the theory of permanent revolution. From this moment on Trotsky and Lenin fought side-by-side. The Party was won over to Lenin's position and Trotsky led the fusion of the Bolsheviks and his own organisation, the Mezhrayontsi, or the Inter-District group.

Still the old Bolsheviks were stuck in the past and unable to make the change, and Lenin found it necessary to fight for his position, as Trotsky explains:

" 'We must abandon the old position', he kept repeating, 'We must make a sharp division between the line of the petty-bourgeoisie and the wage-worker' ". (See Trotsky's *History of the Russian Revolution*, Vol. 1 page 301).

The result was an outburst of subjective resentment from the old Bolsheviks:

"The Old Bolsheviks – who pretentiously emphasised this appellation in April 1917 - were condemned to defeat because they were defending exactly that element of the party tradition which had not passed the historic test. 'I belong to the old Bolshevik Leninists', said Kalinin, for instance, at the Petrograd conference of April 14, 'and I consider the old Leninism has not by any means proved good-for-nothing in the present peculiar moment, and I am astonished at the declaration of Comrade Lenin that the old Bolsheviks have become an obstacle at the present moment.' Lenin had to listen to many offended voices in those days. However in breaking with the traditional formula of the Party Lenin did not in the least cease to be a Leninist. He threw off the worn-out shell of Bolshevism in order to summon its nucleus to a new life" (*Op. Cit.* page 305)

The "old Bolsheviks" under Stalin's influence were eventually shamed into submission. Bitterly resenting Trotsky, with whom Lenin, from this moment, fought side by side, they meekly submitted to Lenin and went along with the Revolution, but were never really convinced, particularly the capricious Stalin, and worse still even the Revolution itself never convinced him. Stalin ended his life as he began it, a died in the wool pedant and counter-revolutionary, and along the way, as we know, he committed all the atrocities necessary to anyone holding such a position, including the murder of Trotsky. A period of historical turmoil separates the Revolution from the death of Trotsky; here we shall only attempt to establish its essence. Siting the experience of the French Revolution Trotsky summed it up as follows:

"It is sufficiently well known that every revolution up to this time has been followed by a reaction, or even a counter-revolution. This, to be sure, has never thrown the nation all the way back to its starting point, but it has always taken from the people the lion's share of their conquests. The victims of the first reactionary wave have been, as a general rule, those pioneers, initiators, and instigators who stood at the head of the masses in the period of the revolutionary offensive. In their stead people of the second line, in league with the former enemies of the revolution, have been advanced to the front. Beneath this dramatic duel of 'coryphées' on the open political scene, shifts have taken place in the relation between classes, and, no less important, profound changes in the psychology of the recently revolutionary masses." (*Revolution Betrayed,* page 88, New Park Publications)

The form taken by this process in the Soviet Union was the rise of the brutally reactionary Stalinist dictatorship as the "second line", so called "old Bolsheviks", Cadets, Mensheviks, Social Revolutionaries and sundry bourgeois riff-raff for whom Lenin's revolutionary theory was incomprehensible. Then at this point Lenin became ill, and although he cut off all political relations with Stalin he was unable to continue in the leadership of the Revolution and died in 1924. Trotsky, now left to fight the counter-revolution alone formed the Left Opposition which, we now know, was ultimately defeated by the Stalinist reaction to the Revolution.

By now Stalin had complete control of the Party and state apparatus, both of which had synthesised into a murderous dictatorship acting with impunity for the material interests of the second line, a bourgeois layer which proceeded to use the state machinery to secure power and privilege for itself. The changes in the psychology of this social layer amounted to acceptance of the new property relations as long as they could be turned to their advantage. What of the fate of the masses? Continuing his parallel with the French Revolution Trotsky explains:

"A revolution is a mighty devourer of human energy, both individual and collective. The nerves give way. Consciousness is shaken and characters are worn out. Events unfold too swiftly for the flow of fresh forces to replace the loss. Hunger, unemployment, the death of the revolutionary cadres, the removal of the masses from administration, all this led to such a physical and moral impoverishment of the Parisian suburbs that they required decades before they were ready for a new insurrection." (*Ibid.*)

The revolutionary cadres who led the Russian Revolution, morally spent by the demands of the Revolution itself, were mostly destroyed by the civil war they were obliged to fight. The masses, exhausted and psychologically broken by the First World War, the civil war against the invading imperialist armies, and the famine and starvation that followed, could now do nothing but fight for survival and that meant accepting the rule of the dictatorship. In 1924 Stalin finally turned his back on the Revolution by declaring his policy of building "socialism in one country" on the basis of "peaceful co-existence" with the imperialist world that encircled his. Trotsky was expelled from the Party and sent into exile in 1929, and the Left Opposition was smashed, its members arrested exiled or murdered.

Unfortunately for Stalin, however, matters did not rest there. Peaceful co-existence can only work if both sides agree, so to secure peace from the imperialists he had to reciprocate by ensuring that the Revolution did not extend beyond the borders of the Soviet Union. This meant betraying the Revolution wherever in raised it head, so by means of political intrigue, false political theories and assassination where necessary, he secured the defeat of the revolutionary struggles in China in

1927, Germany in 1933, Spain in 1935, and ended by signing a pact of non-aggression with Hitler in 1940.

And even more unfortunately for Stalin, Trotsky continued to lead the forces of the Left Opposition in other countries, with its headquarters in Paris and his son Leon Sedov as secretary of its Bureau. It must have been at this point that Stalin finally resolved to have Trotsky murdered, and we can begin to trace out the answer to the crucial question we posed above, how did the assassin penetrate Trotsky's organisation and get to his intended victim?

The Penetration

The man who led the whole operation for Stalin was Mark Zborowsky. He left the Soviet Union in 1921 for Poland, and from there travelled to France. By his own account given years later, testifying before a US Senate Sub-Committee in 1956, he was first approached by the GPU in 1933 and asked to infiltrate the Left Opposition headquarters in Paris and report back. This he achieved in 1936, worming his way into Sedov's confidence as a secretary and writing for the Left Opposition publication, *The Bulletin*.

His first job for the GPU was to help their agents in Paris steal Trotsky's Russian archives from the International Institute of Social History in Paris. Next, he gained access to all correspondence, including all correspondence between Sedov and Trotsky after he arrived in Mexico in 1937. Then in February 1928 Sedov was admitted to a Russian émigré hospital run by Stalinist sympathisers suffering abdominal pains and died under mysterious circumstances. With hindsight it is clear that Zborowski was involved in a plot to take his life, since he later admitted that he had reported that Sedov was in the hospital to his GPU controllers. But still he was trusted, and when the Fourth International was founded in 1938 he was appointed representative of the Russian Section. Now it was time for his most important assignment, to oversee the assassination of Trotsky. The man for the job, it seems, had already been selected, Jac Monard alias Ramon Mercader, an experienced hit-man who had been operating with Stalinist murder gangs during the Spanish civil war.

Zborowski introduced Mercader into the Paris organisation, but the job of getting him to his intended victim had to be organised from the United States, where Stalinist agents were already in place. When a member of the American Trotskyist party, the Socialist Workers Party, Sylvia Ageloff, decided to take a trip to Europe they saw their chance. Out of the blue Ageloff received a phone call from an old acquaintance, Ruby Weil, who had joined the Communist Party. She said that she was going to Europe too, and offered to travel together. When they both arrived in Paris, Weil introduced Ageloff to Mercader, who immediately went to work, setting up a relationship with Ageloff, and they arranged for him to come the America. Mercader duly arrived in September 1939 travelling on a false passport under the name of Frank Jacson. No doubt he reported immediately to the GPU boss in America, Dr. Gregory Robinowitz, present in New York posing as the head of the Russian Red Cross organisation. Within days he told Ageloff that he had found a job with the Allied Purchasing Commission in Mexico.

Once there Jacson/Mercader went to work in the time-honoured manner, visiting Trotsky's house, offering written work for publication, making his car available, ingratiating himself. Then he made his move - he organised the armed raid on Trotsky's house on 24 May referred to above. There can be no doubt that he was involved, since it was later discovered that he had rented a room in an office building together with the leader of the raid, David Siqueiros, a leader of the Mexican Stalinist party. This having failed we can be sure that Mercader's GPU bosses were incensed and told him the get the job done at the risk of his own life, which explains his desperate act the following August.

Above we remarked that the plot to murder Trotsky appears as a bloody trail from the Kremlin right up to Trotsky's study. It is important to understand this, because Trotsky was not just a man, he was a living historical principle, the incarnation of the struggle for world social revolution against the "old Bolshevik", Stalinist reaction. It is doubly important to understand this because it explains what happened next. It is abundantly clear what *should* have happened. The situation at the house should have been meticulously examined and the security arrangements throughout the Fourth International should have been reviewed. A crash training programme in security practice should have begun immediately. But the answer to the question "what happened next" is this; nothing – absolutely nothing! In spite of their direct responsibility in the matter neither Hansen nor the SWP carried out any investigation, and there is no record of any changes in organisation or practice as a result of these catastrophic lapses in security.

One circumstance got in the way – the Second World War. But this only meant that it was very difficult for sections of the newly founded Fourth International outside the United States to get involved. The organisation in the United State, however, the Socialist Workers Party, had nothing in its way and what is more was directly involved, and the man at the very centre of it all, Joseph Hansen, was ideally placed to address all these issues, but nothing was done. After the war the Fourth International was divided into factions each claiming the title. Hansen's section was the United Secretariat, and the British section, the Workers Revolutionary Party, was the leading section of the International Committee of the Fourth International, (ICFI). Then in 1975 this organisation, during its ongoing investigations into the death of Trotsky, discovered previously unpublished State Department documents to show that Hansen had secret meetings with the FBI and the GPU immediately prior to the assassination. One of these documents was a letter from Robert G. McGregor, a senior member of the FBI and US Consul General in Mexico, one of whose responsibilities was the investigation of "communist activities", to his superiors in the US State Department. Dated 1 September 1940. It reads:

The Truth Comes to Light

"Hansen stated that when in New York in 1938 he was himself approached by an agent of the GPU and asked to desert the Fourth International and join the Third. He referred the matter to Trotsky who asked him to go as far with the matter as possible. **For three months Hansen had relations with a man who identified himself as 'John' and did not otherwise reveal his identity.**" (See *News Line* 11 January 1977)

"John" was Dr. Gregory Rabinowitz, the head of the GPU organisation in America. Even if Trotsky did know about this, which seems unlikely, why has Hansen never revealed that he was having such meetings with the American authorities and the GPU? It is crucial information in any investigation into the murder of Trotsky. Even if only to ensure his own personal integrity, Hansen would surely have been most anxious to fully report such activity to his organisation and to the working class, and it would have been crucial information for the political education of his party and the International.

Letters released by the State Department show that Hansen made further visits to the US embassy in Mexico immediately after the assassination, asking to be put in touch "confidentially" with the State Department in Washington, "in order to investigate into Trotsky's assassination", and was put in touch with an FBI agent, J. Little. Hansen never reported any of this to the SWP leaders, and certainly their respected leader, James P. Cannon, never knew; it was at best an act of crass political ignorance or at worst outright treachery. Clearly the FBI was as pleased as anyone that Trotsky was dead and had no intention of inquiring into the matter. The FBI was already investigating the SWP in preparation to making mass arrests under the recently passed Alien Registration Act. Twenty-eight members were arrested in December 1941, but significantly Hansen was not among them. Who grassed them up?

All these operations against the Fourth International were made possible by a catastrophic penetration by the GPU. The Headquarters of the Socialist Workers Party, the most important section of the Fourth International, was in New York. The leader of this party was James P. Cannon, and his personal secretary was Sylvia Caldwell. In 1950 she was exposed as a GPU agent in the Fourth International. On November 11th. 1950, Louis Budenz, a leader of the American Stalinist Communist Party, submitted a sworn affidavit to the Un-American Activities Committee. He gave a detailed account of his collusion with the GPU in helping to infiltrate the Trotskyist movement in the United States, and focused on the role of Sylvia Caldwell.

> "Another person whom I introduced to Roberts [an alias of Dr. Gregory Rabinowitz] was Sylvia Caulwell [*sic*] and whose maiden name was something like Sylvia Kallen."

Kallen and Franklin were other names used by Caldwell. Her role was further exposed on November 29, 1960 – and this time it made front page news all over the United States. On that day the US Government arrested Dr. Robert Soblen of New York as a Soviet Spy and named Sylvia Kallen (Caldwell) as one of his co-conspirators. It finally emerged that Caldwell worked as a GPU agent from 1938 to 1947, handing over all the internal documents of the SWP to her GPU controller.

The ICFI published all this material in 1974, but the main leaders of the Socialist Workers Party, Joseph Hansen and George Novak, denied all the evidence and fiercely defended Franklin/Caldwell. In the November 24, 1974 issue of *Intercontinental Press*, Hansen wrote:

> "Sylvia Caldwell, (that was her party name), worked very hard in her rather difficult assignment of managing the office of the Socialist Workers Party, which included helping Cannon in a secretarial capacity. In fact all the comrades who shared these often irksome chores with her regarded her as exemplary. They burned as much as she did over the slander spread by Budenz."

Later the SWP leader, James P. Cannon, also inexplicably came to her defence, but there was no question of slander. Budenz had given this evidence to a Congressional Committee in a sworn affidavit and the evidence against Caldwell in the Soblen case was later confirmed by a Grand Jury. How can we explain Hansen's and Novack's behaviour? Clearly Caldwell was a GPU agent who had opened the doors wide to the GPU assassin and they were covering up for her.

Yet another security lapse must have come to Hansen's attention. In 1956 none other than Mark Zborowski, now living in America, hit the front pages when the FBI questioned him on suspicion of spying activities for the GPU, now renamed the KGB, from the early 1930's. This means that he was a GPU agent in the Trotskyist movement before, during, and after the death of Trotsky. He was now working as professor of anthropology at a top university. He was of course known to Hansen as Etienne, the man who had been present at the Paris Head Quarters of the Left Opposition and the founding of the Fourth international. He later went to prison for five years having committed perjury at the trial of another GPU agent, Jack Soble. Of course Hansen knew of Zborowski's involvement with Mercader and the plot to kill Trotsky, since Sylvia Agelof had given this information at a Senate-Sub-committee enquiry in 1950, but neither he nor his organisation had anything to say about this devastating news.

But the penetration of Hansen's organisation was not confined to the GPU-KGB, it was the FBI as well. In October 1976 George Vereeken, the Belgian Trotskyist leader, revealed in a special edition of his paper, *Pouvoir aux Travaileurs,* that the US Attorney-General had issued a statement saying that there "were 66 FBI agents active in the American Socialist Workers Party, together with 1,300 occasional informers not belonging to them." Vereeken further reports:

"On 15 September 1976 the US Prosecutor-General ordered the FBI to cease surveillance activity in the Socialist Workers Party (SWP) and Young Socialist Alliance (YSA) of which Hansen and Novack are the main leaders. This surveillance, which has lasted for 38 years, is now too costly and has become pointless. These organisations are no longer a danger to state security. The *Militant,* organ of the SWP, says that 'certain officials at the Department of Justice in Washington are, according to some sources, worried that if the 66 informers all leave at once, there is a risk of them being identified.'"

What an indictment on a "Trotskyist" party – "it is no longer a danger to state security"!

No investigation of these breaches of security was ever carried out by the American Socialist Workers Party, nor did it make any attempt, at any time, to investigate the Murder of Trotsky. Clearly, it was their duty to do so since its leader, Joseph Hansen, was responsible for Trotsky's personal security at Coyoacan. As we shall see this turned out to be not just carelessness or incompetence, but deliberate suppression of investigation of security lapses in the Trotskyist movement, a serious case of which occurred in 1974.

In August of that year a serious situation was brought to the attention of the Central Committee of the Workers League, the American Trotskyist organisation which had fraternal ties with the ICFI. It was reported that Nancy Fields, a member of the League and personal associate of National Secretary Tim Wohlforth, had family ties with the CIA, and had been carrying out seriously disruptive practices and closing down branches of the League. The National Committee took the view that this was a serious breach of security, the most important aspect being that Wohlforth was aware of Fields' connection with the CIA and had failed to report it.

The National Committee voted unanimously that Wohlforth and Fields should be suspended pending an investigation, their own votes included. However one month later, September 29th, they both refused to co-operate with the inquiry, resigned from the League and Wohlforth joined the SWP. Hansen, of whom Wohlforth had been seriously critical in the past, now sprang to the Defence of Wohlforth. What this meant, in effect, was that no proper investigation within the Workers League could be carried out; Hansen had succeeded is suppressing it. However, the long process of investigation by the ICFI now reached a climactic conclusion. The full significance of all the facts uncovered by the ICFI had revealed the real truth of why there had been no proper investigation into the assassination of Trotsky. Those responsible for the crime had not, as might have been expected, departed the scene of the crime – they had stayed in place to cover it up. Even Zborowski had not gone away. On the basis of this conclusion the ICFI decided to bring matters to a head. On January 1, 1976, the International Committee of the Fourth International issued the following indictment against Joseph Hansen and his comrade in the SWP George Novack with comprehensive supporting evidence:

> "After painstaking research in Europe and America, the International Committee presents an irrefutable indictment of both men and calls for a public inquiry along the lines of the Dewey Commission of 1937 with a tribunal including worldwide representatives of the Trotskyist movement. *International Committee of the Fourth International, January 1ˢᵗ. 1976"* (See *How the GPU Murdered Trotsky*, Large format, ISBN 0 902030 78 7)

During the following months the British section of the ICFI published many articles in its daily paper, *News Line,* accusing Hansen of complicity with the GPU and the FBI and insisting on the need for a full inquiry, and Hansen replied in his publication, *Intercontinental express.* But most of these replies took the form of criticism of the man who was undoubtedly the powerhouse behind the struggle for attention to security matters, Gerry Healy, not on the security question but along political and philosophical lines, while the need for any investigation into security lapses was dismissed and those who insisted on it were accused of being "paranoid". Here is the essence of the matter. Whatever the actual circumstances, whatever the rights and wrongs, the history of the Fourth

International is one of the most devastating damage done by agents of the GPU-KGB and the capitalist states which Hansen had ignored and suppressed.

During the course of the investigation many documents were published accusing Hansen and Novak of complicity in such hostile incursions, to which they made lengthy evasive replies. (See references below). Such is the quantity of this material that an attempt to analyse it all would require volumes and would, in the final result, remain my own account. The matter can only be decided by a lengthy commission of inquiry according to the method chosen by Trotsky himself years earlier. Let everybody have their say, let everybody submit evidence and have the opportunity to challenge that presented by others. Until then the most convincing and damning indictment presented by the ICFI must stand unanswered. What honest Trotskyist, faced with such an accusation, would not insist, *absolutely insist*, on and international commission of inquiry to clear his or her name?

Hansen and Novack, and every other organisation claiming allegiance to Trotsky, have fiercely resisted this, and this in itself is a serious indication of guilt. However, at some point those under suspicion decided to strike back. On 14th. January 1977 they organised a meeting in the Friends Meeting House in London to strike what they hoped would be a decisive blow at the ICFI. Led by Tariq Ali of the revisionist International Marxist Group it was attended by the leaders of virtually all the Trotskyist groups in the world. To their surprise however, the leader of the whole ICFI investigation, Gerry Healy, entered the hall and sat quietly in the audience. By now however, since there could be no logical or credible refusal to participate in the ICFI proposal for a commission of inquiry, they could do nothing but falsify the record and divert attention from the main questions. To this end they intensified their personal attack of Healy, who sat patiently listening to a tirade of false accusation for two hours, at the end of which he narrowly lost a vote on his request to speak in reply.

There is no further record of any real inquiry into the murder of Trotsky, and that begs the obvious question, why not? Disinterestedness or carelessness might be understood, but a positive record of opposition must surely be an indication of actual state control of such organisations. It does seem, as we have suggested, that those guilty of Trotsky's murder remained at the scene of the crime to cover it up. But there is one more most significant event in the struggle for the world party of social revolution. It is clear from the historical record that the only organisation which took a serious position on security questions was the ICFI and its British section Workers Revolutionary Party. All the others positively opposed proper security practice. Then, in 1985, came a very significant development. The WRP, the only organisation with a serious approach to security as we have shown, suffered catastrophic disruption at the hands of state provocateurs. It emerged that all its considerable material assets had been embezzled by un-principled cliques of disgruntled members. Under the machinations of the leaders of these cliques, obviously state provocateurs, the Party exploded into a series of splits and within a year it ceased to exist.

Some of the truth behind this emerged two years later. In 1987, Peter Write's book, *Spycatcher*, was published, revealing the kind of MI5 operations which prepared the split. "We burgled and bugged our way across London with impunity", he boasts, and explains that in 1981 MI5 had undergone reorganisation and preparation to concentrate its attention on the labour movement:

"Early in his tenure as Director-General, [of MI5 – TB.], Hanley called a meeting to discuss the changing shape of MI5's priorities. The meeting began with a presentation by Hanley on the climate of subversion in the country, and the growth of what he called the 'far and wide left'. The Prime Minister and the Home Office, he said, had left him in no doubt that they wanted a major increase in effort on this target. He handed over to a young and ambitious F Branch officer, David Ransome, who outlined the activities and structure of a host of left-wing splinter groups, like the Workers Revolutionary Party and the Socialist Workers Party." (Page 359-60)

This meeting took place in 1981, shortly after Margaret Thatcher came to power. Four years later, the WRP, the only organisation with a serious approach to security as we have shown, suffered catastrophic disruption at the hands of state provocateurs. Surely this begs the question: Why the WRP, the only organisation concerned with security, but not a single one of the organisations positively opposed to such measures? Carelessness we can understand, but why were they positively opposed? And why do they find favour with the capitalist state? Only a commission of inquiry could have answered these questions, and it still can and must.

Conclusion

It is here then that the story of the assassination of Leon Trotsky rests – for now. The necessity now is to bring this historical lesson to future generations as widely and comprehensively as possible. There can be no thought of continuing Trotsky's struggle to build the world party of social revolution without training new cadres of working class youth in the spirit of this historical struggle. The irrefutable conclusion must be drawn. The existing "Trotskyist" organisations appear to have been seriously penetrated by state agents of the ruling class, and the struggle to build the international party of world social revolution must begin anew with completely fresh forces.

References

News Line, daily paper of the Workers Revolutionary Party from 1974

Gerry Healy, A Revolutionary Life, Corinna Lotz and Paul Feldman, Lupus Books, ISBN 0 9523454 0 4

How the GPU Murdered Trotsky, New Park Publications (Includes Hansen's replies) ISBN 0 86151 019 4

Website, The Gerry Healy Archive, www.gerryhealy.net

The GPU in the Trotskyist Movement, George Vereeken, New Park Publications

The Mind of an Assassin, Isaac Don Levine, Weidenfeld &Nicolson

Our Own People, Elisabeth K. Poretsky, Oxford University Press, SBN 472-73500-4

-oOo-

Trotsky Explains the Dialectic

When Trotsky arrived in Mexico in January 1937 the Socialist Workers Party of America, led at that time by James P. Cannon, became his main base of support. It was a bad situation: The theoretical life of the Party had no firm basis in dialectical materialist theory and there was a struggle in progress between the majority of the central committee and a minority who openly opposed and rejected the dialectic. The opposition, led by James Burnham and Max Shachtman, represented the typically American philosophical method of pragmatism. Trotsky briefly determines this type of theory as follows:

> "Pragmatism, a mixture of rationalism and empiricism, became the national philosophy of the United States. The theoretical methodology of Max Eastman in not fundamentally different from the methodology of Henry Ford – both regard living society from the point of view of an 'engineer' (Eastman – platonically). Historically the present disdainful attitude toward the dialectic is explained simply by the fact that the grandfathers and great grandmothers of Max Eastman and others did not need the dialectic in order to conquer territory and enrich themselves. But times have changed and the philosophy of pragmaticism has entered a period of bankruptcy just as has American capitalism." (*In Defence of Marxism*, New Park Publications, page 57)

Pragmaticism is a bourgeois subjective idealist philosophy which determines the value of knowledge gained from experience by its practical utility at the individual level. While this outlook met the needs of individuals during the period of expansion of American capitalism during the days of continuous territorial expansion and population increase due to massive immigration, it could give no true reflection of the contradictions of the more developed capitalism of the 1930's. Notwithstanding its continued existence to this day, Trotsky's assertion that American capitalism was bankrupt was quite correct. Like a bankrupt who succeeds in concealing his predicament by continuing to secure credit, American capitalism has stayed on its feet since the 1930's by dollar inflation and bank credit. Pragmaticism had "entered a period of bankruptcy" because this truth could not be grasped and understood on the basis of such philosophy.

Criticising an article Burnham and Shachtman wrote in the Party publication, *New International*, in January 1939, Trotsky writes, "The authors of the article did not show, could not and did not care to show, this internal connection between philosophy and the material development, and frankly explained why." He goes on to quote from the article:

> " 'The two authors of the present article', they wrote of themselves, 'differ thoroughly on their estimate of the general theory of dialectical materialism, one of them accepting it and the other rejecting it ... There is nothing anomalous in such a situation. Though theory is doubtless in one way or another related to practice, the relation is not invariably direct or immediate; and as we have before had occasion to remark, human beings often act inconsistently. From the point of view of each of the authors there is in the other a certain such inconsistency between philosophical theory and political practice, which might on some occasion lead to decisive concrete disagreement. But it does not now, nor has anyone yet demonstrated that agreement or disagreement on the more abstract doctrines of dialectical materialism necessarily affects today's or tomorrows concrete

practical issues – and political parties, programmes and struggles are based on concrete issues. We all may hope that as we go along or when there is more leisure, agreement may also be reached on the more abstract questions. Meanwhile there is fascism and war and unemployment." (Page 57)

Trotsky immediately wrote to Shachtman in reply to the article, informing him that "the section on the dialectic is the greatest blow that you, personally, as editor of the *New International*, could have delivered to Marxist theory." He went on the explain political mistakes that flowed from this theoretical position, particularly with respect to the nature of the Stalinist regime and the Soviet Union. However, so disastrous was the theoretical mistake that Trotsky was obliged to explain the dialectical materialist method from the most basic principles, and the result was the following exposition of Marxist theory, unique in its combination of depth and clarity. We give his explanation here in full:

The ABC of Materialist Dialectics

Gangrenous sceptics like Souvarine believe that 'nobody knows' what the dialectic is. And there are 'Marxists' who kowtow reverently before Souvarine and hope to learn something from him. And these Marxists hide not only in the *Modern Monthly*. Unfortunately a current of Souvarinism exists in the present opposition in the SWP. And here it is necessary to warn young comrades: Beware of this malignant infection!

The dialectic is neither fiction nor mysticism, but a science of the forms of our thinking insofar as it is not limited to the daily problems of life but attempts to arrive at an understanding of more complicated and drawn-out processes. The dialectic and formal logic bear a relationship similar to that between higher and lower mathematics.

I here attempt to sketch the substance of the problem in a very concise form. The Aristotelian logic of the simple syllogism starts from the proposition that 'A' is equal to 'A'. This postulate is accepted as an axiom for a multitude of practical human actions and elementary generalisations. But in realty 'A' is not equal to 'A'. This is easy to prove if we observe these two letters under a lens – they are quite different from each other. But, one can object, the question is not of the size or the form of the letters, since they are only symbols for equal quantities, for instance, a pound of sugar. The objection is beside the point; in reality a pound of sugar is never equal to a pound of sugar – a more delicate scale always discloses a difference. Again one can object; but a pound of sugar is equal to itself. Neither is this true – all bodies change uninterruptedly in size, weight, colour, etc. They are never equal to themselves. A sophist will respond that a pound of sugar is equal to itself 'at any given moment.' Aside from the extremely dubious practical value of this 'axiom', it does not withstand theoretical criticism either. How should we really conceive the word 'moment'? If it is an infinitesimal interval of time, then a pound of sugar is subjected during the course of that 'moment' to inevitable changes. Or is the 'moment' a purely mathematical abstraction, that is, a zero of time? But everything exists in time; and existence itself is an uninterrupted process of transformation; time is consequently a fundamental element of existence. Thus the axiom 'A' is equal to 'A' signifies that a thing is equal to itself if it does not change, that is, if it does not exist.

At first glance it would seem that such 'subtleties' are useless. In reality they are of decisive significance. The axiom 'A' is equal to 'A' appears on one hand to be the point of departure of all our knowledge, on the other hand the point of departure for all the errors in our knowledge. To make use of the axiom 'A' is equal to 'A' with impunity is possible only within certain *limits*. When quantitative changes in 'A' are negligible for the task at hand then we can assume that 'A' is equal to 'A'. That is, for example, the manner in which a buyer and a seller consider a pound of sugar. We consider the temperature of the sun likewise. Until recently we considered the buying power of the dollar in the same way. But quantitative changes beyond certain limits become converted into qualitative. A pound of sugar subjected to the action of water or kerosene ceases to be a pound of sugar. A dollar in the embrace of a president ceases to be a dollar. To determine at the right moment the critical point where quantity changes into quality is one of the most important and difficult tasks in all the spheres of knowledge including sociology.

Every worker knows that it is impossible to make two completely equal objects. In the elaboration of bearing-brass into cone bearings, a certain deviation is allowed for the cones which should not, however, go beyond certain limits (this is called tolerance). By observing the norms of tolerance, the cones are considered as being equal. ('A' is equal to 'A'). When the tolerance is exceeded the quantity goes over into quality; in other words, the cone bearings become inferior or completely worthless.

Our scientific thinking is only a part of our general practice including techniques. For concepts there also exists 'tolerance' which is established not by formal logic issuing from the axiom 'A' is equal to 'A', but by the dialectical logic issuing from the axiom that everything is always changing. 'Common sense' is characterised by the fact that it systematically exceeds dialectical 'tolerance'.

Vulgar thought operates with such concepts as capitalism, morals, freedom, workers' state, etc., as fixed abstractions, presuming that capitalism is equal to capitalism, morals are equal to morals etc. Dialectical thinking analyses all things and phenomena in their continuous change, while determining in the material conditions of those changes that critical limit beyond which 'A' ceases to be 'A', a workers' state ceases to be a workers' state.

The fundamental flaw of vulgar thought lies in the fact that it wishes to content itself with motionless imprints of a reality which consists of eternal motion. Dialectical thinking gives to concepts, by means of closer approximations, corrections, concretisation, a richness of content and flexibility, I would even say a succulence which to a certain extent brings them close to living phenomena. Not capitalism in general, but a given capitalism at a given stage of development. Not a workers' state in general, but a workers' state in a backward country in an imperialist encirclement, etc.

Dialectical thinking is related to vulgar thinking in the same way as a motion picture is related to a still photograph. The motion picture does not outlaw the still photograph but combines series of them according to the laws of motion. Dialectics does not deny the syllogism, but teaches us to combine syllogisms in such a way as to bring our understanding closer to the eternally changing reality. Hegel in his *Logic* established a series of laws: change of quantity into quality, development through contradictions, conflict of content and form, interruption of continuity, change of possibility into inevitability, etc. which are just as important for theoretical thought as is the simple syllogism for more elementary tasks.

Hegel wrote before Darwin and before Marx. Thanks to the powerful impulse given to thought by the French Revolution, Hegel anticipated the general movement of science. But because it was only an *anticipation*, although by a genius, it received from Hegel an idealistic character. Hegel operated with ideological shadows as the ultimate reality. Marx demonstrated that the movement of these ideological shadows reflected nothing but the movement of material bodies.

We call our dialectic, materialist, since its roots are neither in heaven nor in the depths of our 'free will', but in objective reality, in nature. Consciousness grew out of the unconscious, psychology out of physiology, the organic world out of the inorganic, the solar system out of nebulae. On all the rungs of this ladder of development, the quantitative changes were transformed into qualitative. Our thought, including dialectical thought, is only one of the forms of the expression of changing matter. There is place within this system for neither God, nor Devil, nor immortal soul, nor eternal norms of laws and morals. The dialectic of thinking, having brown out of the dialectic of nature, possesses consequently a thoroughly materialist character.

Darwinism, which explained the evolution of species through quantitative transformations passing into qualitative, was the highest triumph of the dialectic in the whole field of organic matter. Another great triumph was the discovery of the table of atomic weights and chemical elements and further the transformation of one element into another.

With these transformations (species, elements, etc.) is closely linked the question of classification, equally important in the natural as in the social sciences. Linnaeus' system (18th. century), utilising as its starting point the immutability of species, was limited to the description and classification of plants according to their external characteristics. The infantile period of botany is analogous to the infantile period of logic, since the forms of our thought develop like everything that lives. Only decisive repudiation of the idea of fixed species, only the study of the history of the evolution of plants and their anatomy prepared the basis for a really scientific classification.

Marx, who in distinction from Darwin was a conscious dialectician, discovered a basis for the scientific classification of human societies in the development of their productive forces and the structure of the relations of ownership with constitute the anatomy of society. Marxism substituted for vulgar descriptive classification of societies and states, which even up to now still flourishes in universities, a materialistic dialectical classification. Only through the method of Marx is it possible correctly to determine both the concept of a workers' state and the moment of its downfall.

All this, as we see, contains nothing 'metaphysical' or 'scholastic', as conceited ignorance affirms. Dialectic logic expresses the laws of motion in contemporary scientific thought. The struggle against materialist dialectics on the contrary expresses a distant past, conservatism of the petty-bourgeoisie, the self-conceit of university routinists and … a spark of hope for an after-life.

(Taken from *In Defence of Marxism* by L. Trotsky, New park Publications, page 63.)

-oOo-

Hegel's Doctrine of Essence

Hegel's *Science of Logic* falls into three parts or "moments", the *Doctrine of Being,* the *Doctrine of Essence*, and the *Doctrine of the Notion.* We dealt with the *Doctrine of Being* in Volume I, under the heading Quality and Quantity, since under this heading we dealt with the three moments of Being, Quality, Quantity, and Measure. Here we deal with the three moments of the *Doctrine of Essence*; Essence as Reflection Within Itself, Appearance, and Actuality.

The concept of Essence is common enough; we all use it. Every thing we see, every experience we have, presents us with the necessity to penetrate to its inner truth before we can deal with it or indeed relate to it in any serious way. You can't judge a book by its cover – if you want to know its truth you have to open it and read it, and when we do we often find that its truth can be grasped the more deeply and profoundly the closer we study it. A great literary work must be penetrated deeply, *plumbed to its depths*. In this way we seek the truth, Essence, of all our experiences.

However, to approach the concept of Essence in this way is to remain at the level of vulgar, unscientific thought, and such thought can never penetrate to the real truth of any thing or the world at large. To do that we must understand every thing, the matter of the universe, human society and human thought, in its *movement and life,* movement which manifests laws of motion that were first enunciated correctly by the idealist Hegel and placed on an objective, that is materialist, basis by Karl Marx. We gave these laws in Volume One as follows:

1. The law of the unity and conflict, interpenetration and transformation of opposites

2. The law of the translation of quality into quantity and from quantity back the quality

3. The law of the negation of the negation.

If we do this correctly we shall formulate the necessary theory to build revolutionary organisation which can lead the working class in the struggle for its emancipation and the transformation of society along socialist foundations. We must firstly study Hegel's *Science of Logic,* (we have the Humanity Books edition), in conjunction with Lenin's conspectus of this work, which is contained in Volume 38 of his Collected Works. In accordance with these laws of motion *The Doctrine of Essence* falls into three moments, Essence as Reflection in Itself, Appearance, and Actuality.

1. Essence as Reflection In-Itself

Lenin begins his conspectus of the Doctrine of essence on page 129 of Volume 38 with a quote from Hegel (Page 389 *Science of Logic*)

" 'The truth of Being is Essence ... Being is the immediate. Knowledge seeks to understand that truth which Being, in and for itself, is, and therefore does not halt at the immediate and its determinations, but penetrates through it, assuming that *behind* this Being there is something other than being itself, and that this background constitutes the truth of Being.' " (*Ibid*)

This seems to be self-evident. The term *Being is the immediate* simply means that when we see a thing in the world external to our thought we make a direct connection with that thing and form a sense impression of it, no third thing is involved and it is entirely superficial.

This moment of cognition, where we perceive a thing in the material world external to thought and reflect it as a thought image in sensation, we call the indeterminate beginning, because all we have us a superficial image of the thing, and we have yet to penetrate to its inner truth. For this reason we refer to the thing as it is objective, in the world external to thought, as the thing-in-itself, because the secret of is truth is still locked up inside it.

Lenin continues to quote Hegel:

" 'This cognition is mediated knowledge, for it is not lodged immediately with and in Essence, but begins at an Other, at Being, and has to make a preliminary passage, the passage of transition beyond Being, or rather of entrance into it …' "

"This cognition" is the cognition of the background at which we have now arrived, but it is the background of *this* Being, that is, it is *this* Being which it reflects. It is mediated by *this* Being and is therefore a single moment of Essence.

"This path of knowledge seems to be the 'activity of cognition external to Being … However, this movement is the movement of Being itself ' "

We experience this movement as a mental effort of our own, but in fact we are simply experiencing the movement of Being which is an objective process taking place in the external world. We see in the quote above that Essence is sublated being. The concept of sublation is best understood as it occurs in the *Doctrine of Being*. When a thing is sublated it is cancelled, negated into the past. However although it no longer exists in its original form, it is preserved, transformed into something new. This "movement of Being itself" results in the transformation, sublation, of Being into Essence.

At this point it is necessary to step aside from the process of cognition to explain the nature of movement itself. Nothing of dialectical logic can be grasped without a proper understanding of motion as such. Quoting Hegel again, Lenin explains:

"Something moves, not because it is here at one point of time and there at another, but because at one and the same point of time it is here and not here, and in this here both is and is not. We must grant the old dialecticians the contradiction which they prove in motion; but what follows is not that there is no motion, but rather that motion is *existent* Contradiction itself." (Page 140 Vol. 38)

Motion never ceases. We can see a thing move if we observe it over a sufficient interval of time. But if we see it at one moment it appears not to move, although the contradiction which causes its movement can be reflected in thought. The thing appears as two-sided, a process of change from one thing to its opposite. The "old dialecticians" were the Greeks, particularly Zeno, who tried to prove the all motion is illusion because it was an impossible contradiction. Lenin then notes that:

" 'Essence … is what it is … by virtue of its own infinite movement of Being … 'Absolute Essence *has no determinate being*. Into this, however, it must pass' " (Page 130)

Hegel says that "essence is past – but timelessly past – Being". (*Science of Logic* Page 389). Clearly any thing, Being, is the result of its past – firstly of the original cause of its coming into Being, and then the accumulated effects of everything that has happened to it and has left its trace, and Essence is the summation of all these causes of its present Being. The is the past contained in the present as Essence.

Essence understood as this infinite, ever moving, ever changing Being, is Absolute Essence. However we know that in nature determinate entities come into being and pass away all the time, hence, in nature, absolute Essence, which has no determinate being, must pass into determinate being and become determinate Essence. The thing under discussion is such a finite moment of Being, but so far we have only considered it at a single moment, unconnected with the rest of infinite matter and time. Being limited in this way, Hegel calls "the *unessential*" Lenin makes a note of this:

"i.e., the unessential, seeming, superficial, - vanishes more often, does no hold so 'tightly', does not 'sit so firmly' as 'Essence – the movement of a river – the foam above and the deep currents below. *But even the foam* is a expression of essence. (Page 130)

Hegel calls this *illusory Being,* or *schein,* German for "show", because, separated from its physical context it is like a drop of foam, an insubstantial, temporary thing, unlike the running water below, the real conditions of its coming to be and existence. In Volume 38 we encounter "Semblance" which is the same thing, no doubt due the differences in translation. Next we take an important step to see how this finite thing-in-itself, the *unessential*, becomes the *essential*, that is, enters into its material context, and reflects infinitely past Being, how the foam is an expression of Essence.

"Essence ... contains Semblance within itself, as infinite internal movement ...In this its self-movement

Essence is Reflection. Semblance is the same as Reflection" (Page 133 Vol. 38)

Up to now we have discussed the thing-in-itself as a moment of Semblance within Absolute Essence; now we turn this round and discuss Absolute Essence as infinite motion becoming determinated into finite things-in-themselves, moments of Semblance. As we have explained, this infinite motion does not cease or pause in these moments of Semblance – it lives in each moment as the internal contradiction of Semblance itself, the transition of each thing-in-itself into its opposite, the negative of itself. This movement lives in Semblance as contradiction. These two sides of Semblance, Being and Essence, mutually reflect each other. Semblance is the same a reflection – It is "Essence as Reflection Within Itself". We now see how this becomes reflected outwards in connection with the rest of nature and is transformed from the *unessential* to the *essential*, part of Absolute Essence, which in turn is determinated into further finite moments of Semblance. We all do this quite naturally, even idealists and those trapped in metaphysical thought, but only dialectical materialist thought can provide us with a scientifically based grasp of the world in constant change according to the natural laws of motion we have set out above, firstly the class struggle.

From the quote above we see that "even the foam is an expression of Essence", but we need to be more exact. How do we get from an *expression of Essence* to Essence itself? Lenin sums up his study of Hegel is this respect as follows:

"1. The determination of the concept out of itself [The thing itself must be considered in its relations and in its development];

"2. The contradictory nature of the thing itself, the contradictory forces and tendencies in each phenomenon;

"3. The union of analysis and synthesis. Such, apparently, are the elements of dialectics." (Page 221 Vol.38)

The "concept" is the reflection of the thing-in-itself in thought, the concept of the thing. Each phenomenon is the reflection in thought of the things with which the thing-in-itself appears to be connected and which determines its Essence in some way.

Taking things out of the world one at a time is like taking it to pieces in order to understand the relation of the thing-in-itself to each part, and this is *analysis*. But at the same time we are putting them together as the history and Essence of the thing-in-itself in Semblance and this is synthesis. We characterise the whole process as "the union of analysis and synthesis". Hegel refers to the result of this synthesis as a sum and unity of opposites

This quantitative process gives rise to a qualitative leap. Having taken this thing in the present and restored to it it's "timelessly past being" we have transformed the *inessential* to the *essential* Essence. The drop of foam is now to be seen in its real substantial truth, liquid water, part of "the river below".

The thing-in-itself in Semblance is the unity of all the parts of its "timelessly past being", their mutual reflection, absolute Essence. But this reflection, this Essence, is internal to the thing itself, each part mutually reflecting inwardly to every other; it is Essence as reflection in-itself. Lenin makes this note:

"Semblance (that which shows itself) is the *Reflection* of Essence in (it) itself." (Page 133 Vol. 38)

We now know the truth of this thing, the cause of its coming into being and its Essence, but we must now consider its relation to the material world of which it is a part in the *present* moment, and for this we must consider its *outward* reflection.

2. Appearance

Appearance must be seen as the Difference within the Identity of Semblance. As we continue to cognise the external world as a quantitative process Semblance becomes negated into Appearance. Both are a "show" of the Essence, but while Semblance is a show of the thing-in-itself, Appearance is a show of the whole world.

Of course we do not reflect the whole world in thought all at once in a *quantitative* way, but we grasp it in a *qualitative* way, the *unifying* Essence of the whole world in so far as we have taken it comprehensively enough. For the purpose of our revolutionary struggle, we take the present world social situation into account, and we concluded long ago that the Essence of the human condition is the struggle between the classes, the capitalist ruling class and the working class. This Essence in the present is the struggle to overthrow the rule of Global Capitalism. But while Appearance is the appearance of the Essence, it is not the Essence itself, and this must be explained. We have all heard the one about the tree in the forest. If a tree falls in the forest and there is no one there to hear it, does it make a noise?

The consistent idealist will say no; indeed he will tell you that there is not even a tree there, because if there is no one there to perceive it then it doesn't exist. A materialist of the metaphysical school will say yes, because he believes that the world exists independently of human perception. Both are wrong. The tree does exist but it doesn't make a noise. What it does when it falls is to set up a pattern of shock-waves in the air, and these waves impinge on the hearing organ of a living creature and produce the phenomenon of sound in his brain. No ear, no brain, no sound, only shock waves in the air. The same can be said of colour. A red object is certainly not red, it is simply reflecting light waves at a certain frequency. These light waves impinge on the eye and cause the phenomena red in sensation. Clearly then, the World of Appearance, in which we live, is very different to the world of Essence, and this limitation of human perception conditions every experience we have, including our daily experience of the class struggle.

Somehow we must make the leap from the world of Appearance to the world of Essence, and to do that we must first understand the difference between them. Quoting Hegel, Lenin notes as follows:

> "The latter" (thing-in-itself) "is not supposed to contain in itself any determinate multiplicity, and consequently obtains this only when brought under external reflection, but remains indifferent to it. (-The thing-in-itself has colour only in relation to the eye, smell in relation to the nose, and so forth)" ... A thing has the Property of effecting this or that in an Other, and of disclosing itself in a peculiar manner in its relation to it ... The thing-in-itself thus exists essentially ..." (Page 149 Vol. 38)

We see a thing, say a trade union leader. He tells us that he will lead us in a heroic fight for our rights – while at the same time taking favours from employers. In one relation he is one thing, but in another he is determined differently. This is the same with all things. While a bank is lending you money it is taking someone else's house. The totality of all such relations Hegel calls Existence. "We shall reserve for Existence all such Being that is mediated", he remarks. In order to penetrate through appearance to Essence, therefore, we must discover the essential inter-connections of our world, the world of global capitalism and the class-struggle at the international level.

Firstly, we notice from experience that certain relations appear with such consistent regularity that we can predict them and even rely on them to advantage. If we push something it will always move in the desired direction. Objects will always fall to the ground or rest satisfactorily on a horizontal surface. The Sun will rise and fall always in the same timespan. Such regular and reliable forms of motion give the concept of *Law*. Wherever certain relations exist there is cause and effect and the result is certain:

> "The movement of the universe in appearances ... in the essentiality of this movement, is law." (Page 152 Vol. 38)

Hence essential Being manifests itself in Appearance, but not directly. In Appearance the Sun rotates round the Earth, but we know that this is the Appearance of the rotation of the Earth about its axis, and the truth is exactly opposite; the Earth rotates about the Sun. From this we can deduce the nature of Appearance. Lenin remarks:

> "The World in and for itself is identical with the World of Appearances, but at the same time is opposite to it. What is positive in one is negative in the other". (Page153, Vol. 38),

There is one more step to take, therefore, before we are truly aware of the world in which we live. We must make the leap to the concept of *Actuality*.

3. Actuality

It is in Actuality that we discover the truth behind Appearance: Not the sound of the falling tree, but the knowledge of the shock wave that cause it. Actuality is the synthesis of Appearance and Essence.

Lenin begins his notes on Actuality with a quote from Hegel as follows:

> "Actuality is the unity of Essence and Existence.
> Sub-divisions: 1) The Absolute – 2) Actuality proper. *Actuality, Possibility,* and *Necessity.* 3) Absolute Relation', *Substance*" (Page 6 Vol. 38, page 529 *Science of Logic*)

This seems a little obscure; certainly Lenin dismisses Hegel's concept of the Absolute in this context. We may take the moments of Actuality to be *Actuality-in-Itself, Possibility and Necessity,* but its relation to *Substance* remains to be explained.

Actuality is the truth of the interrelations of Being, which is in constant motion and change. Since we are speaking of the totality of Being the truth of this motion is Absolute Essence. Such motion and change is the same as development, and this presents infinite *Possibility,* the objective tendency for new Determinate Being to take form.

Possibility rests on the objective existence of all the conditions of a new development to come into Being, but which, at first, do not constitute the positive cause for such new

Being. In the further development of Absolute Essence these same conditions are qualitatively transformed into *Necessity,* that is, *essential,* active cause of new Being. This is a crucial moment for revolutionary political struggle and such moments must never be missed. It is by being conscious of such moments of development of the class struggle that Marxist cadres can swiftly adjust their practice to meet the new conditions, whereas the formal thinker will be caught unawares or miss the moment completely.

The concept of *Substance* is a general understanding of the situation as a changing form. *Substance* is the inner unity of the motion of matter and is the determinate cause of its own motion, a self-sustaining quantity of matter which has its own law of motion. The working class is such a *Substance* because it is driven by the necessity and consciousness of its own unity of action in the necessary forms. Nature consists of such interacting *Substances* as particular forms of the motion of matter.

This is the world in which we first experienced the Identity of the source of our sensation. Having grasped it in the moment of Semblance we must now understand it in this objective context. We do this by placing it back in its proper connections with all the other sides and aspects of the global capitalist system, in the *present,* and in particular as they directly affect us in our class struggle. Phenomena such a bank crises, trade war, actual war, industrial struggles and strikes, political oppression etc., all affect the Actuality of the thing-in itself in Semblance.

Having cognised the real truth of our situation, concretely in the present, we can formulate an idea for practical struggle. Hegel deals with the leap to this moment in the last part of the *Science of Logic, the Doctrine of the Notion.* We shall deal with this in the third volume of this anthology.

Engels on the Identity of Thought and Being

Foreword

Workers who find themselves in the leadership of the struggle against the predations of the ruling class, the intensification of exploitation, ever new oppressive law and destruction of our social services etc., are faced with the constant necessity to explain the underlying reasons for this process to those who take no interest in political matters. We encounter great difficulty, not because these matters are hard to understand, but because we are not the only ones advancing explanations. The ruling class, we know, is pouring out a deluge of false information and "explanation" of the reasons for our rapidly deteriorating conditions of life through all forms of media for every minute of every day and night.

What is necessary, therefore, is not a simple process of direct refutation of the lies and falsehood they pour out, but a process of education that will equip every working class person to make the identity of thought and being and to recognise the falsehood of all capitalist propaganda through their own powers of logical analysis, and to formulate the political outlook upon which to fight for their emancipation. This process was begun in the mid-nineteenth century by Karl Marx and Frederick Engels.

Here we reproduce a limited extract from an important work entitled Ludwig Feuerbach and the End of Classical German Philosophy by Engels, where he deals with the central question of philosophy, the identity of thinking and being, from which all our theoretical efforts must begin, This extract is taken from

44

*the Progress Publishers pamphlet and it begins on page
19. A reading of the whole work is necessary. (TB)*

* * *

The great question of all philosophy, especially of more
recent philosophy, is that concerning the relation of thinking to
being. From the very early times when men, still completely
ignorant of the structure of their own bodies, under the
stimulus of dream apparitions[1] came to believe that their
thinking and sensation were not activities of their bodies, but
of a distinct soul which inhabits the body and leaves it at death
– from this time men have been driven to reflect about the
relation between this soul and the outside world. If upon death
it took leave of the body and lived on, there was no occasion
to invent yet another distinct death for it. Thus arose the idea
of immortality, which at that stage of development appeared
not at all as a consolation but as a fate against which it was no
use fighting, and often enough, as among the Greeks, as a
positive misfortune. The quandary arising from the common
universal ignorance of what to do with this soul, once its
existence had been accepted, after the death of the body, and
not religious desire for consolation, led in a general way to the
tedious notion of personal immortality. In an exactly similar
manner the first gods arose through the personification of
natural forces. And these gods in the further development of
religions assumed more and more extramundane form, until
finally by a process of abstraction, I might almost say of
distillation, occurring naturally in the course of man's
intellectual development, out of the many more or less limited
and mutually limiting gods there arose in the minds of men the
idea of one exclusive God of the monotheist religions.

Thus the question of the relation of thinking to being, the
relation of spirit to nature – the paramount question of the

whole of philosophy – has, no less than all religion, its roots in the narrow-minded and ignorant notions of savagery. But the question could for the first time be put forward in its whole acuteness, could achieve its full significance, only after humanity in Europe had awakened from the long hibernation of the Christian Middle Ages. The question of thinking in relation to being, a question which, by the way, had played a great part also in the scholasticism of the Middle Ages, the question; which is primary, spirit or nature – the question, in relation to the church, was sharpened into this: Did God create the world or has the world been in existence eternally?

The answers which the philosophers gave to this question split them into two great camps. Those who asserted the primacy of spirit to nature and, therefore, in the last instance, assumed world creation in some form or other – and among the philosophers, Hegel for example, this creation becomes still more intricate and impossible than in Christianity – comprise the camp of idealism. The others, who regarded nature as primary, belong to the various schools of materialism.

These two expressions, idealism and materialism, originally signify nothing but this; and here too they are not used in any other sense. What confusion arises when some other meaning is put into them will be seen below.

But the question of the relation of thinking and being has yet another side; in what relation do our thoughts about the world surrounding us stand to the world itself? Is our thinking capable of the cognition of the real world? Are we able in our ideas and notions of the real world to produce a correct reflection of reality? In philosophical language this question is called the question of the identity of thinking and being, and the overwhelming majority of philosophers give an affirmative answer to this question. With Hegel, for example, its affirmation is self-evident; for what we cognise in the external world is precisely its thought content – that which makes the world a gradual realisation of the absolute idea, which absolute idea has existed somewhere from eternity, independent of the world and before the world. But it is manifest without further proof that thought can know a content which is from the outset a thought content. It is equally manifest that what is to be proved here is already tacitly contained in the premises. But that in no way prevents Hegel from drawing the further conclusion from his proof of the identity of thinking and being that his philosophy, because it is correct for his thinking, is therefore the only correct one, and that the identity of thinking and being must prove its validity by mankind immediately translating his philosophy from theory into practice and transforming the whole world according to Hegelian principles. This is an illusion which he shares with well-night all philosophers.

In addition there is yet a set of different philosophers – those who question the possibility of any cognition, or at least an exhaustive cognition, of the world. To them, among the more modern ones, belong Hume and Kant, and they have played a very important role in philosophical development. What is decisive in the refutation of this view has already been said by Hegel, in so far as this was possible from an idealist standpoint. The materialistic additions made by Feuerbach are more ingenious than profound. The most telling refutation of this as of all other philosophical crotchets is practice, namely, experiment and industry. If we are able to prove the correctness of our conception of a natural process by making it ourselves, bringing it into being out of its conditions and making it serve our own purposes into the bargain, then there is an end to the Kantian ungraspable "thing-in-itself". The chemical substances produced in the bodies of plants and animals remained just such "things-in-themselves" until organic chemistry began to produce them one after another, whereupon the "thing-in-itself" became a thing-for-us, as, for instance, alizarin, the colouring matter of the madder, which we no longer trouble to grow in the madder routes in the field, but produce much more cheaply and simply from coal tar. For three hundred years the Copernican solar system was a hypothesis with a hundred, a thousand or ten thousand chances to one in its favour, but still always a hypothesis. But when Leverrier, by means of data provided by this system, not only deduced the necessity of the existence of an unknown planet, but also located the position in the heavens which this planet must necessarily occupy, and when Gaulle actually found this planet,[2] the Copernican system was proved. If, nevertheless, the Neo-Kantians are attempting to resurrect the Kantian conception in Germany and the agnostics that of Hume in England (where in fact it never became extinct), this is, in view of their theoretical and practical refutation accomplished long ago, scientifically a regression and practically merely a shamefaced way of surreptitiously accepting materialism, while denying it before the world.

---

1. Among savages and lower barbarians the idea is still universal that the human forms which appear in dreams are souls which have temporarily left their bodies; the real man is, therefore, held responsible for the acts committed by his dream apparition against the dreamer. Thus Imthurn found this belief current, for example, among the Indians of Guiana in 1884. (Note by Engels.)

2. The planet referred to is Neptune, discovered in 1846 by Johann Galle, an astronomer at Berlin Observatory.

-oOo-

Philosophical Materialism
Terry Button

"Our sensation, our consciousness, is only an image of the external world, and it is obvious that an image cannot exist without the thing imaged, and that the latter exists independently of that which images it." (V.I. Lenin, *Materialism and Empirio-Criticism*, Collected Works Vol. 14, page 51)

The totality of Being consists in a unity of opposites, on one side our body of knowledge and all forms of thought, consciousness, and on the other the world which exists outside our conscious, the material world. The necessity to determine how these two sides of the totality of being relate therefore arises. There are only two possibilities. Where two things relate there are conditions of both unity and conflict between them. In nature, just as we never find a perfect circle or a perfect straight line, so we never find a perfect balance between such a unity; one side must be cause and the other effect.

The relation between thought, consciousness, and the world outside consciousness to which it is related, therefore, must be determined in this way. Which is cause and which effect? Clearly there are only two possibilities, thought is cause and the world outside effect, of vice versa, the world is cause and thought effect. Since there are only two sides there can be no third solution possible; many attempts to find one have been made, but all such solutions amount to nothing but an eclectic muddle of the two. The idea that thought is cause and the world effect we call idealism, and the opposite idea, that the world is cause and thought effect, we call materialism. It is important to stick to these meanings – all other meanings are incorrect usages of the words.

Marxism is a materialist philosophy. In the early part of the twentieth century Lenin found it necessary to conduct a fierce fight against members of the Bolshevik Party who tried to insert muddled idealist ideas into Marxist theory which, they claimed, were based on the latest discoveries of physical science. They named their theory *empirio-criticism,* and Lenin's materialist polemic against them appeared in a book called *Materialism and Empirio-Criticism,* which we find in Volume 14 of his Collected Works.

He goes to great length to show that empirio-criticism is nothing but idealism wrapped up in sophisticated academic language. He begins with a historical account of philosophical idealism, quoting the classical idealist philosopher, Bishop George Berkeley, (1685 to 1753). He quotes a passage from Berkeley's main work, *Treatise Concerning the Principles of Human Knowledge* published in 1710.

"It is indeed an opinion strangely prevailing amongst men, that houses, mountains, rivers, and in a word all sensible objects have an existence, natural or real, distinct from their being perceived by the understanding." This opinion is a "manifest contradiction, for, what are the afore-mentioned objects but things we perceive by sense? And what do we perceive besides our own ideas or sensations? And is it not plainly repugnant that any one of these, or any combination of them, should exist unperceived?" (Lenin's Collected Works, Vol. 14, p.24). A little further on , (page 27), Lenin quotes Berkeley as saying, "if so it shall seem good, use the word 'matter' in the same sense as other men use 'nothing'".

Here is a simple account of the idealist view, nothing exists unless perceived by the mind; it is this very perception that is the cause of its existence. What follows below is a brief explanation of the certainty of the opposite, the materialist view that the world is the cause of thought.

We do not need to repeat here that Marx adopted the dialectical logic of Hegel, but corrected in the light of the materialist philosophy of Ludwig Feuerbach, (*See Ludwig Feuerbach and the End of Classical German Philosophy* by F. Engels) Marx summarised his studies of Feuerbach's writing in ten famous thesis, the second of which is a follows:

"The question of whether objective truth can be attributed to human thinking is not a question of theory but is a practical question. In practice man must prove the truth, that is, the reality and power, the this-sidedness of his thinking. The dispute over the reality or non-reality of thinking which is isolated from practice is purely a scholastic question."

On page 101 of Volume 14 Lenin, quoting from this work, explains Engels' objection to philosophers such a Hume and Kant who deny the knowability of the world:

"The most telling refutation of this as of all philosophical crotchets (Schrullen) is practice, namely, experiment and industry. If we are able to prove the correctness of our conception of a natural process by making it ourselves, bringing it into being out of its conditions and making it serve our own purposes into the bargain, then there is an end to the Kantian incomprehensible 'thing-in-itself'. The chemical substances produced in the bodies of plants and animals remained just such 'things-in-themselves' until organic chemistry began to produce them one after another, whereupon the 'thing-in-itself' became a 'thing-for-us', as, for instance, alizarin, the colouring matter of the madder, which we no longer trouble to grow in the madder roots in the field, but produce much more cheaply and simply from coal tar." (See Lenin collected Works Vol. 14 page 101. Quoted from *Ludwig Feuerbach and the End of Classical German Philosophy* by F. Engels)

Two questions are posed and answered here. 1). Does the natural world exist outside and independently of us? And 2). Can we know its inner truth, its Essence? Lenin answers these fundamental questions as follows:

"What is the kernel of Engels' objection? Yesterday we did not know that coal tar contains alizarin. Today we know that it does. The question is, did coal tar contain alizarin yesterday? Of course it did. To doubt it would be to make a mockery of modern science. And if that is so, three important epistemological conclusion follow:

1) Things exist independently of our sensations, outside of us, for it is beyond doubt that alizarin existed in coal tar yesterday and it is equally beyond doubt that yesterday we knew nothing of the existence of this alizarin and received no sensations from it.

2) There is definitely no difference in principle between the phenomenon and the thing-in-itself, and there can not be any such difference. The only difference is between what is known and what is not yet known. And philosophical inventions of specific boundaries between the one and the other, inventions to the effect that the thing-in-itself is 'beyond' phenomena, (Kant), or that we can and must fence ourselves off by

some philosophical partition from the problem of a world which in one part or another is still unknown but which exists outside us (Hume) - all this is the sheerest nonsense, Schrule, crotchet, fantasy.

3) In the theory of knowledge, as in every other sphere of science, we must think dialectically, that is, we must not regard our knowledge as ready made and unalterable, but must determine how knowledge emerges from ignorance, how incomplete, inexact knowledge becomes more complete and more exact." (Page 102)

Surely the first point requires no further explanation. In any case we know that the world existed long before the possibility of organic life and mental reflection of it. As to the second point, we should explain that the "phenomenon" is the sensuous sensation or image of the thing in the external world in human perception. Lenin says that there is no difference between the phenomenon and the thing-in-itself. This explanation is necessary because some previous philosophers, particularly Emanuel Kant, accepted that the world existed independently of man and our perception of it, but held that we could never know its inner, hidden truth, in philosophical terms, its Essence. The truth of the thing perceived is locked up inside it beyond human reach – it is a "thing-in-itself". He reasoned as follows:

"Transcendental idealism allows that the objects of external intuition – as intuited in space, and all changes in time – as represented by the internal sense, are real ... But time and space, with all appearances therein, are not in themselves things. They are nothing but representations, and cannot exist outside and apart from the mind. (*Critique of Pure Reason*, Everyman books, page 356)

Kant's concept of transcendental idealism simply means the transcendence of the mind, (the ideal), reaching out to embrace the external material world, but for him space and time were things of the mind only and the real conditions of existence of things in the external world could never be known. The truth of a thing remained locked up inside it, it was an unknowable "thing-in-itself". But, says Marx in the second thesis, "in practice man must prove the truth". If we go into practice, and change the thing according to its conditions of existence, the truth is revealed; we find the alizarin in the coal tar. This is the difference between what is known and what is not yet known, what we knew as the thing-in-itself, and the new knowledge arising from practice. That is why we say that practice is the highest point of theory – it transforms the thing-in-itself into the thing-for-us.

One last but crucially important point. Why must thought be dialectical? Because all matter is interconnected and in motion and manifests certain laws of change and development. Its motion is its truth. If we do not follow this development according to these laws of motion then we are not reflecting the material world in thought properly according to its own nature. Our thought will not be truly materialist and we shall never formulate correct theory as a guide to practice.

Terry Button October 2019

-oOo-

Workers Control and the State

Articles have appeared in *Socialist Appeal,* fortnightly paper of the Marxist International Tendency, dealing with the conception of "workers control" and planned "socialist" economy, a discussion current among class conscious workers. These concepts are universally misunderstood, and the views expressed in *Socialist Appeal* only perpetuate and deepen this misunderstanding. On page 13 of *Socialist Appeal* for 19 September 2019 we read:

> "The real problem is one of ownership. As the old adage goes: 'you can't plan what you can't control, and you can't control what to don't own'. How can a Labour Government have control of the economy without taking over the banks and major monopolies?"

Clearly, to pose the question as to how a Labour government could control the economy without taking over the banks implies the possibility that it might take them over. This is dangerously misleading: *We can be absolutely certain the no Labour government would ever do any such thing.*

As we shall see, the "real problem" has nothing to do with ownership, and in any case if a Labour government "took over" the banks and big monopolies it still would not "own" their assets and we would still not have socialism and we still could not plan. Finally, as we shall see, there is no such thing as "socialism" as a *quality*, a finished system. In order to untangle this muddle we must start from the need to *control*, and we certainly *can* control the economy without owning it.

There really is no need for confusion on these questions, Lenin spelled it all out in a number of publications. The necessity for control, of course, stems from the need to plan, to combat the appalling disruption of the capitalist world and national economy, and national planning is clearly a function of the state, so first we must understand the nature of the state under which we live. Summing up Engels' exposition of the capitalist state in The *Origin of the Family, Private Property and the State*, Lenin writes:

> "This expresses with perfect clarity the basic idea of Marxism with regard to the historical role and meaning of the state. The state is a product and a manifestation of the *irreconcilability* of class antagonisms. The state arises where, when and in so far as class antagonisms objectively *cannot* be reconciled. And, conversely, the existence of the state proves that the class antagonisms are irreconcilable." (*The State and Revolution*, Collected Works Vol. 25, page 392)

The key thing is to grasp that the state regulates society riven by *irreconcilable* class antagonisms, hence social stability can only be achieved by *violent oppression* of one class by the other. Lenin continues to quote Engels:

> "Because the state arose from the need to hold class antagonisms in check, but because it arose, at the same time, in the midst of the conflict of these classes, it is, as a rule, the state of the most powerful, economically dominant class, which, through the medium of the state, becomes also the politically dominant class, and thus acquires the new means of holding down and exploiting the oppressed class ..." The ancient feudal states were organs for the exploitation of the slaves and serfs; likewise, "the modern representative state is an instrument of exploitation of wage labour by capital." (*Op. Cit.* page 397)

Here we have the solution to Sewell's muddle above. If the working class must impose its own solution to the irreconcilable antagonisms of the capitalist class system, (state control and economic planning), then it must first *smash* the capitalist state and *impose one of its own.* It must become the ruling class. Lenin explains the nature of the state that rules over us:

> "Engels elucidates the concept of the 'power' which is called the state, a power which arose from society but places itself above it and alienates itself more and more from it. What does this power mainly consist of? It consists of special bodies of armed men having prisons, etc., at their command." (*Op. Cit* page 394)

In order for the working class to take control of the economic life of the nation, therefore, it must first smash the power which enforces the existing, capitalist class relations. That will almost certainly be a very violent struggle, a revolution in which state power passes from the capitalist class to the workers, the proletariat, a civil war which promises to be a very bloody affair. But nowhere does Sewell say anything about this; nor, for that matter, have I ever seen this question mentioned in *Socialist Appeal.* Lenin makes it crystal clear:

> "This is precisely what is meant by 'abolition' of the state as state. This is precisely the 'act' of taking possession of the means of production in the name of society". (Vol 25, page 402.)

The period following the revolution, the political rule of the working class, we call the *dictatorship of the proletariat,* and it is only here that the imposition of workers control begins, because such control is unthinkable without the necessary means of coercion, a state consisting of armed bodies of men with prisons etc. at their disposal. Now we see the true nature of this concept, workers control. It does not mean workers on the board of this or that company, the workers, one way or another, determining the activities of an enterprise, setting wage levels etc. It means the control of the entire *capitalist economy* by the *workers' state,* as system of violent coercion made necessary due to the irreconcilable antagonisms between the classes. Not the workers directly, but the workers *through their state.* A moments thought shows that planning is out of the question on any other basis. Exactly what form it will take cannot at this stage be known but we can be quite sure that Parliament will be abolished and replaced by a soviet system. We shall, to the amazement of the likes of Sewell, be *controlling what don't own,* because at this stage the economy will be just as capitalist as it was the day before the revolution, owned by shareholders, banks etc., and wage labour. Now begins the socialist period, as Lenin explains, quoting from the *Poverty of Philosophy* by Karl Marx.

> "The proletariat will use its political supremacy to wrest, by degrees, all capital from the bourgeoisie, to centralise all instruments of production in the hands of the state, i.e., of the proletariat organised as the ruling class; and to increase the total of productive forces as rapidly as possible." (*Op. cit.* page 407)

The key here is the term "by degrees". Socialism is *not* a finished social and economic structure, a *qualitative* identity in its own right, as is commonly supposed, but a *quantitative* process of development through time. The unfolding of the national plan means the progressive nationalisation of banks, main industries etc. It is an interim stage, the process of transition from capitalism to communism, from class divided society to classless society. Socialism will have done its job the day it ceases to exist.

What property relations will remain? No concrete predictions can be made, but we can expect the means of production and distribution to be in the hands of some kind of guiding body, a freely united association of some kind, without the need for means of violent coercion, no longer a state. Looking ahead to this moment it is usual to refer to such property relations as "public ownership", but this remains a contradictory term. What everybody owns, *nobody* owns. It seems that a new term will be needed once we have experience of this as yet unknown situation. Certainly the working class will own nothing because the concept of property itself will have passed into history, and the concept of the working class and class divided society as such will have gone with it.

There remains one last crucial question. What has happened to the state? Lenin gives the answer with a quote from *Anti-Düring* by Engels:

"As soon as there is no longer any social class to be held in subjection, as soon as class rule, and the individual struggle for existence based upon the present anarchy of production, with the collisions and excesses arising from this struggle, are removed, nothing more remains to be held in subjection – nothing necessitating a social coercive force, a state. The first act by which the state really comes forward as a representative of the whole of society – the taking possession of the means of production in the name of society – is also its last independent act as a state. State interference in social relations becomes, in one domain after another, superfluous, and then dies down of itself. The government of persons is replaced by the administration of things, and by the conduct of processes of production. The state is not 'abolished'. *It withers away*. This gives the measure of the value of the phrase 'a free peoples state', both as to its justifiable use for a time from an agitational point of view, and as to its ultimate scientific insufficiency; and also of the so-called anarchists demand that the state be abolished overnight." (Quoted by Lenin in *The State and Revolution*, Collected Works Vol. 25, page 400)

Lenin takes great care to explain that Engels speaks here of the *workers' state,* the proletariat organised as the ruling class, once the workers have won "the battle for democracy", that is, they have overthrown the capitalist state by revolutionary means. It is the workers' state, the dictatorship of the proletariat, that withers away, *not* the capitalist state, which, since it is an organisation of repression by violence. must be overthrown and smashed by violent revolution. In this way democracy is maintained and preserved at a higher level, sublated into a new form, *true democracy for the people*, not confined to a minority exploiting class.

-oOo-

The Logic of *Capital*

"That the method employed in *Das Kapital* has been little understood, is shown by the various conceptions, contradictory one to another, that have been formed of it." (Quoted by Karl Marx from the Paris *Review Positiviste,* in *Capital* Volume 1, page 17)

It is universally believed that Marx took the single commodity as the starting point for his analysis of capitalist political economy, but this is not the materialist way.

"The wealth of those societies in which the capitalist mode of production prevails, presents itself as 'an immense accumulation of commodities,' its unit being a single commodity." (Page 35)

So, we see, he *didn't* start with the single commodity, but with capitalist society as a *whole,* and analysed this system into its parts, commodities. In this way he understood the commodity as the expression of a *social relation*, and it is the change and development of this social relation which the subject of the whole three volume work. (This is the Marxist way; see the addendum below).

Next, famously, he took this part of the whole, the commodity, out of its objective connections in the whole and analysed it into its sides or aspects:

"A commodity is, in the first place, an object outside us, a thing that by its properties satisfies human wants of some sort or another."

If it satisfies a human want, then it must reflect that want in some way. It is the world external to thought, the living context from which it is abstracted, that determines its quality. "Every useful thing, as iron, paper, &c., may be looked at from the two points of view of quality and quantity". (*Ibid.*)

Here we have the other side of Marx's method, dialectical logic. Quality is determinate being, finite Identity. Quantity, Hegel informs us, is the form of being which is "indifferent the Quality", is indeterminate, infinite, living change itself. On the basis of the materialist understanding of the world Engels formulated the three laws of the science of Marxism:

1. All progress takes place through the unity and conflict, inter-penetration and transformation of opposites.

2. The law of the transformation of quality and quantity and of quantity back to quality.

3. The law of the negation of the negation.

These are the universal laws of nature, governing the *whole* of nature in its historical development, whether chemical processes, biological processes, mechanical motion, human society or human thought. We shall attempt to trace through Marx's analysis of the commodity in the light of these laws. We should bear in mind that it is only the fact that they meet as opposites in unity and conflict in the act of exchange that determines them as commodities in the first place.

"In the form of society we are about to consider, they are, in addition, the material depositories of exchange value ... Exchange-value, at first site, presents itself as a quantitative relation, as the proportion in which values in use of one sort are exchanged for those of another sort, a relation constantly changing with time and place." (Page 36)

These two commodities, each a two-sided relation of quality and quantity, come into unity and conflict of opposites in the moment of exchange, the social act of their owners. It is the *qualities* which bring them together because each commodity owner requires to take possession, and make use of, the other's commodity as a use value. However, their physical properties as use values are not in any way related by the amount of time and effort required to produce them, and each commodity owner is now concerned only with this. The commodities to be exchanged are now understood as *quantities*: In accordance with the first law, quality has been transformed into quantity.

They begin to bargain, as a quantitative process through time, and they do so until a satisfactory rate of exchange is reached. What each requires is a sufficient return for the time and effort spent in the production of his commodity. If the exchange is to take place, each owner must be equally satisfied, and this, we know, is happening a million times every day everywhere things are produced for exchange. Marx give us examples; "a dozen watches, yards of linen, tons of iron."

We can now begin to grasp this process as a case of the dialectical laws of motion we have given. The two opposites, the commodities to be exchanged, are in *unity* through their qualities, but in *conflict* through their different quantities of labour time. A unity of two different quantities is a *ratio*, and the resolution of the quantitative struggle between any two opposites in conflict, the leap from quantity to quality, takes place at the critical ratio as determined by the quantities of the qualities in unity and conflict. This is called the moment of Measure. In the case of the exchange of commodities, the ratio is always 1:1, since an equal measure of labour time must be exchanged. In the examples given by Marx, he implies that a watch contains 1/12 of the labour time contained in a ton of iron, since 12 watches contains the same amount.

So we have explained the first law, the nature of the unity and conflict of opposites. We have explained the first part of the second law, the transformation of Quality into Quantity. However, when something is transformed in this way we call it a Negation, because the first moment, the things as Quality, is now a thing of the past, rendered null, and they are now, so far as the owners are concerned things of quantity.

But as we have explained, this quantitative process is in its own turn negated by the leap back to Quality with the completion of the exchange, negating, rendering the quantitative process past, null, thus completing the second law, and this is a negation of a negation. Now the owners are concerned with the *quality* of the commodities, their *use value*.

It is the second negation, the negation of the first negation, which makes the leap to a new Quality not just a moment of change but in a general way a moment of development to a higher, more complex form of motion. Both of the opposites are carried forward and contained in the result in synthesised form as its past history.

But, having resolved the contradiction contained in the act of exchange, we immediately encounter another. Since each commodity is a different quality, the labour process contained in each as quantity must have been qualitatively different. How can they be identical in the moment of Measure?

Above we have said that quantity is the determination that is indifferent to quality. Quantity taken abstractly can be a quantity of *any* quality, but taken concretely it must be a quantity of *some* quality. It is at this moment that we must return the part which we have taken from the whole, the commodity from is social context, and return it to the whole, capitalist society from which we began. Marx does this next:

"Some people might think that if the value of a commodity is determined by the quantity of labour spent on it, the more idle and unskilled the labourer, the more valuable would his commodity be, because more time would be required in its production. The labour, however, that forms the substance of value, is homogeneous human labour, expenditure of one uniform labour power. The total labour-power of society, which is embodied in the sum total of the values of all commodities produced in that society, counts here as one homogeneous mass of human labour-power, composed though it be of innumerable individual units. Each of these units is the same as any other, so far as it has the character of the average labour-power of society, and takes effect as such; that is, so far as it requires for the production of a commodity, no more time than is needed on average, no more that is socially necessary. The labour time socially necessary is that required to produce an article under the normal conditions of production, and with the average degree of skill and intensity prevalent at the time. The introduction of power looms into England probably reduced by one half the labour required to weave a given quantity of yarn into cloth. The hand loom weavers, as a matter of fact, continued to require the same time as before, but for all that, the product of one hour of their labour represented after the change one half an hour's social labour, and consequently fell to one-half of its former value." (Page 39)

So we have adopted the correct dialectical materialist approach to Marx's work. We began materialistically from the whole, a mass of commodities. We took the commodity out of its social context and analysed it and discovered its internal contradiction according to the dialectical laws of motion of nature, including human society and human thought. Finally we placed it back in its social context and in doing so discovered its inner truth, its dialectical Essence, average social labour. *Capital* can never be understood unless it is seen as a process which takes place in this way. As Lenin explains:

"It is impossible to completely understand Marx's *Capital*, especially its first chapter, without having thoroughly studied and understood the whole of Hegel's Logic. Consequently, half a century later none of the Marxists understood Marx!" (*Collected Works* Volume 38, page 180)

It is no accident that the work comprises three volumes. Why three? Did it just happen to amount to three when Marx put down his pen? Certainly not. The whole work is an expression of the laws we have given, the laws of the Science of Marxism. The first volume was Quality, a society determined by the exchange of private property in the form of commodities. But this system changes quantitatively, large sums of wealth being accumulated as the private property of a small number of individuals. This quantitative process reaches a qualitative leap in the second volume, where the trade in commodities is negated into the trade in these large sums of wealth – the circulation of capital as a commodity. The third volume negates this negation by synthesising the two moments into a new whole, the logical history of capitalism to date, laying bare the law of its development as a finite historical epoch.

Addendum

The following is taken from *Socialism: Utopian and Scientific* by Frederic Engels: The page number will vary according to the publication

"When we consider and reflect upon Nature at large or the history of mankind or our own intellectual activity, at first we see the picture of an endless entanglement of relations and reactions, permutations and combinations, in which nothing remains what, where and as it was, but everything moves, changes, comes into being and passes away. We see, therefore, at first the picture as a whole, with its individual parts still more or less kept in the background; we observe the movements, transitions, connections, rather than the things that move, combine or are connected. This primitive, naïve but intrinsically correct conception of the world is that of ancient Greek philosophy, and was first clearly formulated by Heraclitus: everything is and is not, for everything is fluid, is constantly changing, constantly coming into being and passing away.

But this conception, correctly as it expresses the general character of the picture of appearances as a whole, does not suffice to explain the details of which this picture is made up, and so long as we do not understand these, we have not a clear idea of the whole picture. In order to understand these details we must detach them from their natural or historical connection and examine each one separately, its nature, special causes, effects, etc. This is, primarily, the task of natural science and historical research: branches of science which the Greeks of classical times, on very good grounds, relegated to a subordinate position, because they had first of all to collect materials for these sciences to work upon. A certain amount of natural and historical material must be collected before there can be any critical analysis, comparison, and arrangement in classes, orders and species. The foundations of the exact natural sciences were, therefore, first worked out by the Greeks of the Alexandrian period, and later on, in the Middle Ages, by the Arabs. Real natural science dates from the second half of the fifteenth century, and thence onward it had advanced with constantly increasing rapidity. The analysis of Nature into its individual parts, the grouping of the different natural processes and objects in definite classes, the study of the internal anatomy of organic bodies in their manifold forms – these were the fundamental conditions of the gigantic strides in our knowledge of Nature that have been made during the last four hundred years. But this method of work also left us as legacy the habit of observing natural objects and processes in isolation, apart from their connection with the vast whole; of observing them in repose, not in motion; as constants, not as essentially variables; in their death, not in their life. And when this way of looking at things was transferred by Bacon and Locke from natural science to philosophy, it begot the narrow, metaphysical mode of thought peculiar to the last century."

-oOo-

The Dialectical 'Cell' of Nature and Capitalism

By
Gerry Healy

Foreword
This article appeared in the *News Line*, daily paper of the Workers Revolutionary Party on 9 June 1981. It is based on Healy's notes for a series of public lectures, the fifth lecture in the series. (TB)

In his article, *On the Question of Dialectics*, (Volume 38, Lenin's *Collected Works*, page 359), Lenin describes the dialectical method as follows:

'Thus in any proposition we can (and must) disclose as in a "nucleus" ("cell") the germs of all the elements of dialectics, and thereby show that dialectics is a property of all human knowledge in general.'

He went on to explain what this 'cell' was all about by referring to the way in which Marx carried out his analysis of *Capital*.

'In his *Capital*, Marx first analyses the simplest, most ordinary and fundamental, most common and everyday relation of bourgeois, (commodity), society, a relation encountered billions of times, vis, the exchange of commodities. In this very simple phenomenon, (in the 'cell' of bourgeois society) analysis reveals all the contradictions (or the germs of all the contradictions) of modern bourgeois society.'

Firstly, we will reveal the dialectical 'cell' of all human knowledge in general and then go on to examine a commodity as the cell of bourgeois society.

One of the forms of reflecting the external world in the mind is through the use of scientific concepts developed by Hegel and rescued from his objective idealist method by Marx. This is explained in his book, *Economic and Philosophical Manuscripts of 1844*, in the chapter on the critique of the Hegelian dialectic. The main object of these concepts is to single out in thought the objects which are nearest to us, from the standpoint of cognition and practice.

'Concepts', wrote Lenin, 'are the highest product of the brain which is the highest product of matter.' (Vol. 38, page 167). On page 136 of the same book he explains the use of concepts as follows:

'Concepts must be hewn, treated, flexible, mobile, relative, mutually connected, united in opposites, in order to embrace the world.'

Through the method of conceptual analysis we set out to reproduce the dialectical world of the real from the dialectical movement of thought.

The Activity of Cognition

Living perception begins with external reflection. It is essential to be clear on the dialectical role of reflection if we are to train our senses to use it to the best advantage. When we speak of the development of thought through reflection we must in fact acknowledge that the source of sensation leading to thought is in the external world around us.

When we reflectively apprehend the external world we establish contact through sensation. This is a universal objective moment of being which denotes the unity between man and the world, established through external reflection. The abstract image of that moment of unity through sensation appears in the mind as Semblance. It is an objective moment of the world as a whole, which means that Semblance too is objective. It is the starting point of new thoughts whose materiality exists in the external world. This is registered in our mind through sensation and appears in the form of an abstract thought image.

Semblance is a reflective moment which emerges as the category of Essence, simply denoting 'self-identity', (page 135, Vol. 38 Lenin's *Collected Works*). It has a two fold character which can best be described as an example of a ray of light starting from the external world, reflected into man and through him into its counterpart, the external world. In his explanation of Semblance, Lenin quotes Hegel approvingly:

'Thus Semblance is Essence itself, but Essence in a determinatedness, and this in such a manner that determinatedness is only its moment. Essence is the showing of itself in itself.' (Page 133, Vol. 38, *Collected Works*.)

And again ... 'Essence contains Semblance within itself, as an infinite internal movement ... In this its self movement Essence is Reflection. Essence is the same as Reflection.' (*Ibid*.)

Hegel explains the contradiction within Essence as 'mere pairs of co-Relatives' not yet absolutely reflected in themselves, hence in Essence the actual unity of the Notion (opposites) is not realised, but only postulated by reflection.

Essence is Being which is starting to mediate about itself through the self-related abstract image of itself.

Hegel speaks of this stage as 'Being coming into mediation with itself', through the negation of itself (Semblance – Essence) – 'other' to which Being is now opposed in its own reflected self. Instead of Being and nought, we now have the terms Positive and Negative. The former as Identity and the latter showing itself as Difference.

These can be described as a pair of correlative terms in reciprocal relationship as opposites, moving from Essence of the lower to Essence of the Higher. The difference between them is implicitly the 'essential difference' between positive and negative. The positive is identical self-relation in such a way as not to be the negative. Their difference lies in their opposition to one another.

Although a definite tendency such as either Positive or Negative may in a complex situation be altered by contact with other tendencies, it still has truth, despite these modifying influences. Positive and negative is stamped, as it were, with a characteristic of its own, only in relation to its other; the one is only reflected into itself as it is into its own other. In this relation they are explicitly the same. Either one can annul the other and itself.

As a difference, essential difference is only the difference of essential difference from itself. As Trotsky explained in *In Defence of Marxism*, (Page 65, New Park edition);

'Every worker knows that it is impossible to make two completely equal objects. In the elaboration of bearing brass into cone bearings, a certain deviation is allowed for the cones which should not, however, go beyond certain limits, (this is called tolerance). By observing the norms of tolerance, the cones are considered as being equal. ("A" is equal to "A"). When the tolerance is exceeded the quantity goes over into quality; in other words, the cone bearings become inferior or completely worthless.

'Our scientific thinking is only a part of our general practice including techniques. For concepts there also "tolerance" which is established not from formal logic issuing from the axiom "A" is equal to "A" but by the dialectical logic issuing from the axiom that everything is always changing.'

The 'Cell' in Dialectical Thought.

The positive produces its own negative which polarises into a further negative for a new positive. These constitute the twin correlative terms in transition into essence of the higher order. The identity of the positive with its negative in unity with difference as negative of the new positive is revealed as ground.

The transition of difference into contradiction is through the incorporation of the movement of the twin correlative opposites as the source of the contradiction.

The build-up of these contradictory properties within essence of the higher order creates the conditions for essence itself to be formed in the concept of appearance. The positive and negative correlative terms now emerge as form (whole) and content (part). The abstract unity and identity of opposite correlative terms appear now as the whole within the part, and completes the dialectical 'cell' in thought. It is this process to which Lenin refers when he explains that:

'Dialectics is the teaching which shows how opposites can be and how they happen to be (how they become) identical – under what conditions they are identical, becoming transformed into one another.' (Page 109. Vol. 38, Lenin's *Collected Works*)

The dialectical cell in thought appears in this abstract unity and identity of opposites as the property of 'all human knowledge in general'.

The Commodity as a Cell

Dialectical concepts reflect the movement of matter in the objective world. If we retrace this development in relation to commodity production then we shall be able to appreciate the Hegelian influence in Marx's *Capital*.

'Human concepts are subjective', stressed Lenin, quoting Hegel, 'in their abstractness, separateness, but objective as a whole, in the process, in the sum total, in the tendency, in the source.' (*Op. Cit.* page 208)

The bourgeois economist David Ricardo established that living human labour was the only source of value. This, at the time, represented a considerable advance towards objective truth in the sphere of political economy. His difficulty arose when it came to explaining the contradiction presented by the need to show the origins of profit. Value had become the manifestation of profit and this in turn was the source of the contradiction for Ricardo, which he tried to resolve in thought. In reality profit was part of the newly-created value, and only new labour could create new value. Ricardo tried to make value and profit appear without contradiction.

Marx explained that 'that was simply an attempt to present that which does not exist as in fact existing.' (*Theories of Surplus Value*). That is subordinating and immediately adapting the concrete to the abstract. It seemed to Ricardo that if thought contradicts the facts then the thought should be altered so as to bring it into line with the general appearance of thought, which was immediately given on the surface – a method which is theoretically false. Marx showed that these were necessary contradictions in the object itself, not inexactitudes of determinations.

He showed that surplus value is 'exclusively the product of that part of capital which is expended on wages and converted into living labour, that is called variable capital.'

The contradictions which Ricardo laboured under were not logical ones, (thought interpreting thought), but real contradictions within the object itself. The essence is value but the inner contents of this value is the direct coincidence of two forms that are polar opposites, namely value and use value.

The emergence of the commodity 'cell' as in dialectical thought concepts, has its original source in the external world of Nature. Living perception has to be understood here as the work of human beings. From the sensations created through such work, the objective abstract image is replaced by abstract value, embodied in, say for example, cloth.

The positive is work and the negative is the abstract work contained in the cloth. The abstract work is the negative of the positive which polarises into the negative of the new positive called use-value. Here is the source of the polar opposites, value and use-value. In the transition from essences of the lower, (value), into essence of the higher, (use value), the path of cognition reflects the actual real movement of the process of production. Essence of the lower presents us with the thing-in-itself as value, which in turn becomes a 'thing-for-itself' as use value, its opposite, when it emerges in appearance as exchange value.

These relations which appear in phenomena as relations between things are, on the contrary, relations between human beings – relations between classes through the class struggle. The new labour needed to transform the cloth into say a jacket or a skirt as a use-value, changes value as a form, which appears as cloth, into exchange-value, as the form in which value appears in a jacket or skirt. Use-value appears in its equivalent value form which is money.

The pair of correlative concepts as opposites, viz. value and use-value, are now embodied as a unity of opposites within exchange value. Exchange value, which is the unity of value and use-value, has now become appearance as part which then finds its identity in the external world through the universal equivalent money as the whole within the part.

This is the 'cell' of the commodity. The abstract opposites are use-value and exchange value, whose unity and identity as opposites is embodied in the real world in the form of a commodity which in simple terms is anything of use for sale.

Through money as the equivalent of value the contradiction appears to be overcome, but is transferred to the class struggle.

-oOo-

The Soviet Thermidor

Foreword

The text below is taken from *Revolution Betrayed*, Trotsky's analysis of the conditions prevailing in the Soviet Union under the bourgeois reaction following the Revolution of 1917. His comparison to the month of Thermidor in which the reaction to the great French Revolution was focussed, it instructive. The history of human society is the history of the struggle between classes, an exploiting ruling class and an exploited and oppressed working class, in various historical forms.

Such struggles have always been driven by the need for revolutionary social transformation made necessary by developing productive forces which call the exploited class to take ruling power and to transform the relations of production and distribution. Marx has characterised revolution as "the locomotive of history". However, in all historical cases, the old ruling class has succeeded in winning for itself privileged conditions in the new society and bringing the revolutionary process to a standstill and even, to an extent, reversing it. This is the secret of the Stalinist dictatorship that followed the Revolution of 1917. Now that we have Trotsky's analysis before us we can understand this process in sufficient depth to effectively resist reaction to the Revolution history has given us to achieve. A thorough study of *Revolution Betrayed* is absolutely necessary. (TB)

Why Stalin Triumphed
(Revolution Betrayed page 86)

The historian of the Soviet Union cannot fail to conclude that the policy of the ruling bureaucracy upon great questions has been a series of contradictory zig-zags. The attempt to explain or justify this by "changing circumstances" obviously won't hold water. To guide means at least in some degree to exercise foresight. The Stalin faction have not in the slightest degree foreseen the inevitable results of the development; they have been caught napping every time. They have reacted with mere administrative reflexes. The theory of each successive turn has been created after the fact, and with small regard for what they were teaching yesterday. On the basis of the same irrefutable facts and documents, the historian will be compelled to conclude that the so-called "Left Opposition" offered an immeasurably more correct analysis of the processes taking place in the country, and far more truly foresaw their further development.

This assertion is contradicted at first glance by the simple fact that the faction which could not see ahead was steadily victorious, while the more penetrating group suffered defeat after defeat. That kind of objection, which comes automatically to mind, is convincing, however, only to those who think rationalistically, and see in politics a logical argument or a chess game. A political struggle is in its essence a struggle of interests and forces, not of arguments. The quality of the leadership is, of course, far from a matter of indifference for the outcome of the conflict, but it is not the only factor, and in the last analysis is not decisive. Each of the struggling camps moreover demands leaders in its own image.

The February revolution raised Kerensky and Tseretelli to power, not because they were "cleverer" or "more astute" than the ruling czarist clique, but because they represented, at least temporarily, the revolutionary masses of the people in their revolt against the old regime. Kerenski was able to drive Lenin underground and imprison other Bolshevik leaders, not because he excelled them in personal qualifications, but because the majority of the workers and soldiers in those days were still following the patriotic bourgeoisie. The personal "superiority" of Kerensky, if it is suitable to employ such a word in this connection, consisted in the fact that he did not see farther than the overwhelming majority. The Bolsheviks in their turn conquered the petty bourgeois democrats, not through the personal superiority of their leaders, but through a new correlation of social forces. The proletariat had succeeded at last in leading the discontented peasantry against the bourgeoisie.

The consecutive stages of the great French Revolution, during its rise and fall alike, demonstrate no less convincingly that the strength of the "leaders" and "heroes" that replaced each other consisted primarily in their correspondence to the character of those classes and strata which supported them. Only this correspondence, and not any irrelevant superiorities whatever, permitted each of them to place the impress of his personality upon a certain historic period. In the successive supremacy of Mirabeau, Brissot, Robespierre, Barras and Bonaparte, there is an obedience to objective law incomparably more effective than the special traits of the historic protagonists themselves.

It is sufficiently well known that every revolution up to this time has been followed by a reaction, or even a counter revolution. This, to be sure, has never thrown the nation all the way back to its starting point, but it has always taken from the people the lion's share of their conquests. The victims of the first reactionary wave have been, as a general rule, those pioneers, initiators, and instigators who stood at the head of the masses in the period of the revolutionary offensive. In their stead people of the second line, in league with the former enemies of the revolution, have been advanced to the front. Beneath this dramatic duel of the "coryphées" on the open political scene, shifts have taken place in the relations between classes, and, no less important, profound changes in the psychology of the recently revolutionary masses.

Answering the bewildered questions of many comrades as to what has become of the activity of the Bolshevik party and the working class – where is its revolutionary initiative, the spirit of self-sacrifice and plebeian pride – why, in place of all this, has appeared so much vileness, cowardice, pusillanimity and careerism – Rakovsky referred to the life story of the French revolution of the eighteenth century, and offered the example of Babeuf, who on emerging from the Abbaye prison likewise wondered what had become of the heroic people of the Parisian suburbs. A revolution is a mighty devourer of human energy, both individual and collective. The nerves give way. Consciousness is shaken and characters are worn out. Events unfold too swiftly for the flow of fresh forces to replace the loss. Hunger, unemployment, the death of the revolutionary cadres, the removal of the masses from administration, all this led to such a physical and moral impoverishment of the Parisian suburbs that they required three decades before they were ready for a new insurrection.

The axiomlike assertions of the Soviet literature, to the effect that the laws of bourgeois revolutions are "inapplicable" to a proletarian revolution, have no scientific content whatever. The proletarian character of the October revolution was determined by the world situation and by a special correlation of internal forces. But the classes themselves were formed in the barbarous circumstances of tsarism and backward capitalism, and were anything but made to order for the demands of a socialist revolution. The exact opposite is true. It is for the very reason that a proletariat still backward in many respects achieved in the space of a few months the unprecedented leap from a semifeudal monarchy to a socialist dictatorship, that the reaction in its ranks was inevitable. This reaction has developed in a series of consecutive waves. External conditions and events have vied with each other in nourishing it. Intervention followed intervention. The revolution got no direct help from the west. Instead of the expected prosperity of the country an ominous destitution reigned for long. Moreover, the outstanding representatives of the working class either died in the civil war, or rose a few steps higher and broke away from the masses. And thus after an unexampled tension of forces, hopes and illusions, there came a long period of weariness, decline and sheer disappointment in the results of the revolution. The ebb of "plebeian pride"'" made room for a flood of pusillanimity and careerism. The new commanding caste rose to its place upon this wave.

The demobilization of the Red Army of five million played no small role in the formation of the bureaucracy. The victorious commanders assumed leading posts in the local Soviets, in economy, in education, and they persistently introduced everywhere that regime which had ensured success in the civil war. Thus on all sides the masses were pushed away gradually from actual participation in the leadership of the country.

The reaction within the proletariat caused an extraordinary flush of hope and confidence in the petty bourgeois strata of town and country, aroused as they were to new life by the NEP, and growing bolder and bolder. The young bureaucracy, which had arisen at first as an agent of the proletariat, began now to feel itself a court of arbitration between the classes. Its independence increased from month to month.

The international situation was pushing with mighty forces in the same direction. The Soviet bureaucracy became more self-confident, the heavier the blows dealt to the world working class. Between these two facts there was not only a chronological, but a causal connection, and one which worked in two directions. The leaders of the bureaucracy promoted the proletarian defeats; the defeats promoted the rise of the bureaucracy. The crushing of the Bulgarian insurrection and the inglorious retreat of the German workers' party in 1923, the collapse of the Esthonian attempt at insurrection in 1924, the treacherous liquidation of the General Strike in England and the unworthy conduct of the Polish workers' party at the installation of Pilsudski in 1926, the terrible massacre of the Chinese revolution in 1927, and, finally, the still more ominous recent defeats in Germany and Austria – these are the historic catastrophes which killed the faith of the Soviet masses in world revolution, and permitted the bureaucracy to rise higher and higher as the sole light of salvation.

As to the causes of the defeat of the world proletariat during the last thirteen years, the author must refer to his other works, where he has tried to expose the ruinous part played by the leadership of the Kremlin, isolated from the masses and profoundly conservative as it is, in the revolutionary movement of all countries. Here we are concerned primarily with the irrefutable and instructive fact that the continual defeats of the revolution in Europe and Asia, while weakening the international position of the Soviet Union, have vastly strengthened the Soviet bureaucracy. Two dates are especially significant in this historic series. In the second half of 1923, the attention of the Soviet workers was passionately fixed on Germany, where the proletariat, it seemed, had stretched out its hand to power. The panicky retreat of the German Communist Party was the heaviest possible disappointment to the working class in the Soviet Union. The Soviet bureaucracy straightway opened a campaign against the theory of the "permanent revolution", and dealt the Left Opposition its first cruel blow. During the years 1926 and 1927 the population of the Soviet Union experienced a new tide of hope. All eyes were now directed to the East where the drama of the Chinese Revolution was unfolding. The Left Opposition had now recovered from the previous blows and was recruiting a phalanx of new adherents. At the end of 1927 the Chinese revolution was massacred by the hangman, Chiang-kai-shek, into whose hands the Communist International had literally betrayed the Chinese workers and peasants. A cold wave of disappointment swept over the masses of the Soviet Union. After an unbridled baiting in the press and at meetings, the bureaucracy finally, in 1928, ventured upon mass arrests among the Left Opposition.

To be sure, tens of thousands of revolutionary fighters gathered round the banner of the Bolshevik-Leninists. The advanced workers were indubitably sympathetic to the Opposition, but that sympathy remained passive. The masses lacked faith that the situation could be changed by a new struggle. Meantime the bureaucracy asserted: "For the sake of an international revolution, the Opposition proposes to drag us into a revolutionary war. Enough of shake-ups! We have earned the right to rest. We will build the socialist Society at home. Rely on us, your leaders!" This gospel of repose firmly consolidated the apparatchiki and the military and state officials and indubitably found an echo among the weary workers, and still more the peasant masses. Can it be, they asked themselves, that the Opposition is actually ready to sacrifice the interests of the Soviet Union for the sake of a "permanent revolution?" In reality, the struggle had been about the life interests of the Soviet State. The false policy of the International in Germany resulted ten years later in the victory of Hitler – that is, in a threatening war danger from the West. And the no less false policy in China reinforced Japanese imperialism and brought very much nearer the danger in the

East. But periods of reaction are characterised above all by a lack of courageous thinking.

The Opposition was isolated. The bureaucracy struck while the iron was hot, exploiting the bewilderment and passivity of the workers, setting their more backward strata against the advanced, and relying more and more boldly upon the Kulak and the petty bourgeois ally in general. In the course of a few years, the bureaucracy thus shattered the revolutionary vanguard of the proletariat.

It would be naïve to imagine that Stalin, previously unknown to the masses, suddenly issued from the wings full armed with a complete strategical plan. No indeed. Before he felt out his own course, the bureaucracy felt out Stalin himself. He brought it all the necessary guarantees: the prestige of an old Bolshevik, a strong character, narrow vision, and close bonds with the political machine as the sole source of his influence. The success that fell upon him was a surprise at first to Stalin himself. It was the friendly welcome of the new ruling group, trying to free itself from the old principles and from the control of the masses, and having need of a reliable arbiter in its inner affairs. A secondary figure before the masses and in the events of the Revolution, Stalin revealed himself as the indubitable leader of the Thermidorian bureaucracy, as first in its midst.

The new ruling caste soon revealed its own ideas, feelings and, more important, its interests. The overwhelming majority of the older generation of the present bureaucracy had stood on the other side of the barricades during the October revolution. (Take, for example, the Soviet ambassadors only: Troyanovsky, Maisky. Potemkin, Surittz, Khinchuk, etc.) Or at least they had stood aside from the struggle. Those of the present bureaucrats who were in the Bolshevik camp in the October days played in the majority of cases no considerable role. As for the young bureaucrats, they have been chosen and educated by the elders, frequently from among their own offspring. These people could not have achieved the October revolution, but they were perfectly suited to exploit in.

Personal incidents in the interval between these two historic chapters were not, of course, without influence. Thus the sickness and death of Lenin undoubtedly hastened the denouement. Had Lenin lived longer, the pressure of the bureaucratic power would have developed, at least during the first years, more slowly. But as early as 1926 Krupskaya said, in a circle of Left Oppositionists: "If Ilych were alive, he would probably already be in prison." The fears and alarming prophecies of Lenin himself were then still fresh in her memory, and she cherished no illusions as to his personal omnipotence against opposing historic winds and currents.

The bureaucracy conquered something more than the Left Opposition. It conquered the Bolshevik Party. It defeated the programme of Lenin, who had seen the chief danger in the conversion of the organs of the state "form servants of society to lords over society." It defeated all these enemies, the Opposition, the party and Lenin, not with ideas and arguments, but with its own social weight. The leaden rump of the bureaucracy outweighed the head of the revolution. This is the secret of the Soviet's Thermidor.

2. The Degeneration of the Bolshevik Party

The Bolshevik Party prepared and insured the October victory. It also created the Soviet state, supplying it with a sturdy skeleton. The degeneration of the party became both cause and consequence of the bureaucratisation of the state. It is necessary to show at least briefly how this happened.

The inner regime of the Bolshevik party was characterised by the method of *democratic centralism.* The combination of these two concepts, democracy and centralism, is not in the least contradictory. The party took watchful care not only that its boundaries should always be strictly defined, but also that all those who entered these boundaries should enjoy the actual right to define the direction of the party policy. Freedom of criticism and intellectual struggle was an irrevocable content of the party democracy. The present doctrine that Bolshevism does not tolerate factions is a myth of the epoch of decline. In reality the history of Bolshevism is a history of the struggle of factions. And, indeed, how could a genuinely revolutionary organisation, setting itself the task of overthrowing the world and uniting under its banner the most audacious iconoclasts, fighters and insurgents, live and develop without intellectual conflicts, without groupings and temporary factional formations? The farsightedness of the Bolshevik leadership often made I possible to soften conflicts and shorten the duration of factional struggle, but no more than that. The Central Committee relied upon this seething democratic support. From this it derived the audacity to make decisions and give orders. The obvious correctness of the leadership at all critical stages gave it that high authority which is the priceless moral capital of centralism.

The regime of the Bolshevik party, especially before it came to power, stood thus in complete contradiction to the regime of the present sections of the Communist International, with their "leaders" appointed from above, making complete changes of policy at a word of command, with their uncontrolled apparatus, haughty in its attitude to the rank and file, servile in its attitude to the Kremlin. But in the first years after the conquest of power also, even when the administrative rust was already visible on the party, every Bolshevik, not excluding Stalin, would have denounced as a malicious slanderer anyone who should have shown him on a screen the image of the party ten or fifteen years later.

The very centre of Lenin's attention and that of his colleagues was occupied by a continual concern to protect the Bolshevik ranks from the vices of those in power. However, the extraordinary closeness and at times actual merging of the party with the state apparatus had already in those first years done indubitable harm to the freedom and elasticity of the party regime. Democracy had been narrowed in proportion as difficulties increased. In the beginning, the party had wished and hoped to preserve freedom of political struggle within the framework of the Soviets. The civil war introduced stern amendments into this calculation. The opposition parties were forbidden one after the other. This measure, obviously in conflict with the spirit of Soviet democracy, the leaders of Bolshevism regarded not as a principle, but as an episodic act of self-defence.

The swift growth of the ruling party, with the novelty and immensity of its tasks, inevitably gave rise to inner disagreements. The underground oppositional currents in the country exerted a pressure through various channels upon the sole legal political organisation, increasing the acuteness of the factional struggle. At the moment of completion of the civil war, this struggle took such sharp forms as to threaten to unsettle the state power. In March 1921, in the days of the Kronstadt revolt, which attracted into its ranks no small number of Bolsheviks, the Tenth Congress of the party thought it necessary to resort to a prohibition of factions – that is, to transfer the political regime prevailing in the state to the inner life of the ruling party. This forbidding of factions was again regarded as an exceptional measure to be abandoned at the first serious improvement in the situation. At the same time, the Central Committee was extremely cautious in applying the new law, concerning itself most of all lest it lead to a strangling of the inner life of the party.

However, what was in its original design merely a necessary concession to a difficult situation, proved perfectly suited to the taste of the bureaucracy, which had then begun to approach the inner life of the party exclusively from the viewpoint of convenience in administration. Already in 1922, during a brief improvement in his health, Lenin, horrified at the threatening growth of bureaucratism, was preparing a struggle against the faction of Stalin, which had made itself the axis of the party machine as a first step toward capturing the machinery of state. A second stroke and then death prevented him from measuring forces with the internal reaction.

The entire effort of Stalin, with whom at that time Zinoviev and Kamenev were working hand in hand, was thenceforth directed to freeing the party machine from the control of the rank-and-file members of the party. In this struggle for "stability" of the Central Committee, Stalin proved the most consistent and reliable of his colleagues. He had no need to tear himself away from international problems; he had never been concerned with them. The petty bourgeois outlook of the new ruling stratum was his own outlook. He profoundly believed that the task of creating socialism was national and administrative in its nature. He looked upon the Communist International as a necessary evil which should be used so far as possible for the purposes of foreign policy. His own party kept a value in his eyes merely as a submissive support for his machine.

Together with the theory of socialism in one country, there was put into circulation by the bureaucracy a theory that in Bolshevism the Central Committee is everything and the party nothing. This second theory was in any case realised with more success than the first. Availing itself of the death of Lenin, the ruling group announced a "Leninist levy." The gates of the party, always carefully guarded, were thrown wide open. Workers, clerks, petty officials, flocked through in crowds. The political aim of this maneuver was to dissolve the revolutionary vanguard in raw human material, without experience, without independence, and yet with the old habit of submitting to authorities. The scheme was successful. By freeing the bureaucracy from the control of the proletarian vanguard, the "Leninist levy" dealt a death blow to the party of Lenin. The machine had won the necessary independence. Democratic centralism gave place to bureaucratic centralism. In the party apparatus itself there now took place a radical reshuffling of personnel from top to bottom. The chief merit of a Bolshevik was declared to be obedience. Under the guise of a struggle with the Opposition, there occurred a sweeping replacement of revolutionists with *chinovniks*. [Professional governmental functionaries.] The history of the Bolshevik party became a history of rapid degeneration.

The political meaning of the developing struggle was darkened for many by the circumstance that the leaders of all three groupings, Left, Centre and Right, belonged to one and the same staff in the Kremlin, the Politburo. To superficial minds it seemed to be a mere matter of personal rivalry, a struggle for the "heritage" of Lenin. But in the conditions of iron dictatorship social antagonisms could not show themselves at first except through the institutions of the ruling party. Many Thermidorians emerged in their day from the circle of Jacobins. Bonaparte himself belonged to that circle in the early years, and subsequently it was from among former Jacobins that the First Consul and Emperor of France selected his most faithful servants. Times change and the Jacobins with them, not excluding the Jacobins of the twentieth century.

Of the Politburo of Lenin's epoch there now remains only Stalin. Two of its members Zinoviev and Kamenev, collaborators of Lenin throughout many years as émigrés, are enduring ten-year prison terms for a crime which they did not commit. Three other members, Rykov, Bukharin and Tomsky, are completely removed from the leadership, but as a reward for submission occupy secondary posts. And, finally, the author of these lines is in exile. The widow of Lenin, Krupskaya, is also under the ban, having proved unable with all her efforts to adjust herself completely to the Thermidor.

[Footnote; Zinoviev and Kamenev were executed in August 1936 for alleged complicity in a "terroristic plot" against Stalin; Tomsky committed suicide or was shot in connection with the same case; Rykov was removed from his post in connection with the plot; Bukharin, although suspected, is still at liberty. – Translator.]

The members of the present Politburo occupied secondary posts throughout the history of the Bolshevik party. If anybody in the first years of the revolution had predicted their future elevation, they would have been the first in surprise, and there would have been no false modesty in their surprise. For this very reason, the rule is more stern at present that the Politburo is always right, and in any case that no man can be right against the Politburo. But, moreover, the Politburo cannot be right against Stalin, who is unable to make mistakes and consequently cannot be right against himself.

Demands for party democracy were through all this time the slogans of all the oppositionist groups, as insistent as they were hopeless. The above-mentioned platform of the Left Opposition demanded in 1927 that a special law be written into the Criminal Code "punishing as a serious state crime every direct or indirect persecution of a worker for criticism." Instead of this, there was introduced into the Criminal Code an article against the Left Opposition itself.

Of party democracy there remained only recollections in the memory of the older generation. And together with it had disappeared the democracy of the soviets, the trade unions, the co-operatives, the cultural and athletic organisations. Above each and every one of them there reigns an unlimited hierarchy of party secretaries. The regime had become "totalitarian" in character several years before the word arrived in Germany. "By means of demoralising methods, which convert thinking communists into machines, destroying the will, character and human dignity", wrote Rakovsky in 1928, "the ruling circles have succeeded in converting themselves into an unremovable and inviolate oligarchy, which replaces the class and party." Since those indignant lines were written, the degeneration of the regime has gone immeasurably farther. The G.P.U. has become the decisive factor in the inner life of the party. If Molotov in March 1936 was able to boast to a French journalist that the ruling party no longer contains any factional struggle, it is only because disagreements are settled by the automatic intervention of the political police. The old Bolshevik party is dead, and no force will resurrect it.

*   *   *

Parallel with the political degeneration of the party, there occurred a moral decay of the uncontrolled apparatus. The word "sovbour" – soviet bourgeois – as applied to a privileged dignitary appeared very early in the workers' vocabulary. With the transfer to the NEP bourgeois tendencies received a more copious field of action. At the 11th. Congress of the party, in March 1922, Lenin gave warning of the danger of a degeneration of the ruling stratum. It has occurred more than once in history, he said, that the conqueror took over the culture of the conquered, when the latter stood at a higher level. The culture of the Russian bourgeoisie and the old bureaucracy was, to be sure, miserable, but alas the new ruling stratum must take off its hat to that culture. "Four thousand seven hundred responsible communists" in Moscow administer the machine. "Who is leading whom" I doubt very much whether you can say that the communists are in the lead ..." In subsequent congresses, Lenin could not speak. But all his thoughts in the last months of his active life were of warning and arming the workers against the oppression, caprice and decay of the bureaucracy. He, however, saw only the first symptoms of the disease.

Christian Rakovsky, former president of the Soviet of People's Commissars of the Ukraine, and later Soviet Ambassador in London and Paris, sent to his friends in 1928, when already in exile, a brief inquiry into the Soviet bureaucracy, which we have quoted above several times, for it still remains the best that has been written on this subject. "In the mind of Lenin, and in all our minds," says Rakovsky, "the task of party leadership was to protect both the party and the working class from the corrupting action of privilege, place and patronage on the part of those in power, from rapprochement with the relics of the old nobility and burgherdom, from the corrupting influence of the NEP, from the temptation of bourgeois morals and ideologies ... We must say frankly, definitely and loudly that the party apparatus has not fulfilled this task, that it has revealed a complete incapacity for its double role of protector and educator. It has failed. It is bankrupt."

It is true that Rakovsky himself, broken by the bureaucratic repressions, subsequently repudiated his own critical judgements. But the seventy-year-old Galileo too, caught in the vise of the Holy Inquisition, found himself compelled to repudiate the system of Copernicus – which did not prevent the earth from continuing to revolve around the sun. We do not believe in the recantation of the sixty-year-old Rakovsky, for he himself has more than once made a withering analysis of such refutations. As to his political criticisms, they have found in the facts of the objective development a far more reliable support than the subjective stout-heartedness of their author.

The conquest of power changes not only the relation of the proletariat to other classes, but also its own inner structure. The wielding of power becomes the speciality of a definite social group, which is the more impatient to solve its own "social problem", the higher its opinion of its own mission. "In a proletarian state, where capitalist accumulation is forbidden to the members of the ruling party, the differentiation is at first functional, but afterwards becomes social. I do not say it becomes a class differentiation, but a social one ..." Rakovsky further explains: "The social situation of the communist who has at his disposal an automobile, a good apartment, regular vacations, and receives the party maximum salary, differs from the situation of the communist who works in the coal mines, where he receives some fifty to sixty rubles a month." Counting over the causes of the degeneration of the Jacobins when in power – the chase after wealth, participation in government contracts, supplies, etc., Rakovsky sites a curious remark of Babeuf to the effect that the degeneration of the new ruling stratum was helped along not a little by the former young ladies of the aristocracy towards whom the Jacobins were very friendly. "What are you doing, small hearted plebeian? Cries Babeuf. "Today they are embracing you and tomorrow they will strange you." A census of the wives of the ruing stratum in the Soviet Union would show a similar picture. The well-known Soviet journalist, Sosnovsky, pointed out the special role played by the "auto-mobile-harem factor" in forming the morals of the Soviet bureaucracy. It is true that

Sosnovsky, too, following Rakovsky, recanted and was returned from Siberia. But that did not improve the morals of the bureaucracy. On the contrary, that very recantation is proof of a progressing demoralisation.

The old articles of Sosnovsky, passed about in manuscript from hand to hand, were sprinkled with unforgettable episodes from the life of the new ruling stratum, plainly showing to what vast degree the conquerors have assimilated the morals of the conquered. Not to return, however, to past years – for Sosnovsky finally exchanged his whip for a lyre in 1934 – we will confine ourselves to wholly fresh examples from the Soviet Press. And we will not select abuses and so-called "excesses", either, but the everyday phenomena legalised by official social opinion.

The director of a Moscow factory, a prominent communist, boasts in Pravda of the cultural growth of the enterprise directed by him. "A mechanic telephones: 'What is your order, sir, check the furnace immediately or wait?' I answer 'Wait'"* The mechanic addresses the director with enormous respect, using the second person plural, while the director answers him in the second person singular. A disgraceful dialogue, impossible in any cultured capitalist country, is related by the director himself on the pages of Pravda as something entirely normal! The editor does not object because he does not notice it. The readers do not object because they are accustomed to it. We also are not surprised, for at solemn sessions in the Kremlin, the "leaders" and Peoples Commissars address in the second person singular directors of factories subordinate to them, presidents of collective farms, shop foremen and working women, especially invited to receive decorations. How can they fail to remember that one of the most revolutionary slogans in tsarist Russia was to demand for the abolition of the use of the second person singular by bosses in addressing their subordinates!

[*It is impossible to convey the flavour of this dialogue in English. The second person singular is used either with intimates in token of affection, or with children, servants and animals in token of superiority]

These Kremlin dialogues of the authorities with "the people", astonishing in their lordly ungraciousness, unmistakably testify that, in spite of the October revolution, the nationalisation of the means of production, collectivisation, and "the liquidation of the kulaks as a class," the relations among men, and that at the very heights of the Soviet pyramid, have not only not yet risen to socialism, but in many respects are still lagging behind a cultured capitalism. In recent years enormous backward steps have been taken in this very important sphere. And the source of this revival of genuine Russian barbarism is indubitably the Soviet Thermidor, which has given complete independence and freedom from control to a bureaucracy possessing little culture, and has given to the masses the well-known gospel of obedience and silence.

We are far from intending to contrast the abstraction of dictatorship with the abstraction of democracy, and weigh their merits on the scale of pure reason. Everything is relative in this world, where change alone endures. The dictatorship of the Bolshevik party proved one of the most powerful instruments of progress in history. But here too, in the words of the poet, "Reason becomes unreason, kindness a pest." The prohibition of oppositional parties brought after it the prohibition of factions. The prohibition of factions ended in a prohibition to think otherwise than the infallible leaders. The police-manufactured monolithism of the party resulted in a bureaucratic impunity which has become a source of all kinds of wantonness and corruption.

3. The Social Roots of Thermidor

We have defined the Soviet thermidor as a triumph of the bureaucracy over the masses. We have tried to disclose the historic conditions of this triumph. The revolutionary vanguard of the proletariat was in part devoured by the administrative apparatus and gradually demoralised, in part annihilated in the civil war, and in part thrown out and crushed. The tired and disappointed masses were indifferent to what was happening on the summits. These conditions, however, important as they may have been in themselves, are inadequate to explain why the bureaucracy succeeded in raising itself above society and getting its fate firmly into its own hands. Its own will to do this would in any case be inadequate; the arising of a new ruling stratum must have deep social causes.

The victory of the Thermidorians over the Jacobins in the eighteenth century was also aided by the weariness of the masses and the demoralisation of the leading cadres, but beneath these essentially incidental phenomena a deep organic process was taking place. The Jacobins rested upon the lower petty bourgeoisie lifted by the great wave. The revolution of the eighteenth century, however, corresponding to the course of development of the productive forces, could not bring the great bourgeoisie to political ascendancy in the long run. The Thermidor was only one of the stages in this inevitable process. What similar social necessity found expression in the Soviet Thermidor? We have tried already in one of the preceding chapters to make a preliminary answer to the question why the gendarme triumphed. We must now prolong our analysis of the conditions of that transition from capitalism to socialism, and the role of the state in the process. Let us again compare theoretic prophecy with reality. "It is still necessary to suppress the bourgeois and its resistance", wrote Lenin in 1917, speaking of the period which should begin immediately after the conquest of power, "but the organ of suppression here is now the majority of the population, and not the minority as has hereto fore always been the case ... In that sense the state is beginning to die away." In what does this dying away express itself? Primarily in the fact that "in place of special institutions of a privileged minority (privileged officials, commanders of a standing army), the majority itself can directly carry out" the functions of suppression. Lenin follows this with a statement axiomatic and unanswerable: "The more universal becomes the very fulfilment of the functions of the state power, the less need there is of this power." The annulment of private property in the means of production removes the principle task of the historic state – defence of the proprietary privileges of the minority against the overwhelming majority.

The dying away of the state begins, then, according to Lenin, on the very day after the expropriation of the expropriators – that is, before the new regime has had time to take up its economic and cultural problems. Every success in the solution of these problems means a further step in the liquidation of the state, its dissolution in the socialist society. The degree of this dissolution is the best index of the depth and efficacy of the socialist structure. We may lay down approximately this sociological theorem: The strength of the compulsion exercised by the masses in a workers state is directly proportional to the strength of the exploitive tendencies, and inversely proportional to the strength of the social solidarity and general loyalty to the new regime. Thus the bureaucracy – that is, the "privileged officials and commanders of a standing army" - represents a special kind of compulsion which the masses cannot or do not wish to exercise, and which, one way or another, is directed against the masses themselves.

If the democratic soviets had preserved to this day their original strength and independence, and yet were compelled to resort the repressions and compulsions on the scale of the first years, this circumstance might of itself give rise to serious anxiety. How much greater must be the alarm in view of the fact that the mass soviets have entirely disappeared from the scene, having turned over the function of compulsion to Stalin, Yagoda and company. And what forms of compulsion! First of all we must ask ourselves: What social cause stands behind this stubborn virility of the state and especially behind its policification? The importance of this question is obvious. In dependence upon the answer, we must either radically revise our traditional views of the socialist society in general, or as radically reject the official estimates of the Soviet Union.

Let us now take from the latest number of a Moscow newspaper a stereotyped characterization of the present Soviet regime, one of those which are repeated throughout the country from day to day and which school children learn by heart: "In the Soviet Union the parasitical classes of capitalists, landlords and Kulaks are completely liquidated, and thus is forever ended the exploitation of man by man. The whole national economy has become socialistic, and the growing Stakhanov movement is preparing the conditions for a transition from socialism to communism." (*Pravda*, April 4, 1936) The world press of the Communist International, it goes without saying, has no other thing to say on this subject. But if exploitation is "ended forever", if the country is really now on the road from socialism, that is, the lowest stage of communism, to its higher stage, then there remains nothing for society to do but throw off at last the straightjacket of the state. In place of this – it is hard even to grasp this contrast with the mind! – the Soviet state had acquired a totalitarian-bureaucratic character.

The same fatal contradiction finds illustration in the fate of the party. Here the problem may be formulated approximately thus: Why, from 1917 to 1921, when the old ruling classes were still fighting with weapons in their hands, when they were actively supported by the imperialists of the whole world, when the kulaks in arms were sabotaging the army and food supplies of the country, - why was it possible to dispute openly and fearlessly in the party about the most critical questions of policy? Why now, after the cessation of intervention, after the shattering of the exploiting classes, after the indubitable successes of industrialisation, after the collectivisation of the overwhelming majority of the peasants, is it impossible to permit the slightest word of criticism of the unremovable leaders? Why is it that any Bolshevik who should demand the calling of the congress of the party in accordance with its constitution would be immediately expelled, any citizen who expressed out loud a doubt of the infallibility of Stalin would be tried and convicted almost as though a participant of a terrorist plot? Whence this terrible, monstrous and unbearable intensity of repression and the police apparatus?

Theory is not a note which you can present at any moment to reality for payment. If a theory proves mistaken we must revise it or fill out its gaps. We must find out those real social forces which have given rise to the contrast between Soviet reality and the traditional Marxist conception. In any case we must not wander in the dark, repeating ritual phrases, useful for the prestige of the leaders, but which nevertheless slap the living reality in the face. We shall now see a convincing example of this.

In a speech at a session of the Central Executive Committee in January 1936, Molotov, the president of the Council of People's Commissars, declared: "The national economy of the country has become socialistic (applause). In that sense [?] we have solved the problem of the liquidation of classes (applause) However, there still remain from the past "elements in their nature hostile to us", fragments of the former ruling classes. Moreover, among the collectivised farmers, state employees and sometimes also the workers, "petty speculators" [spekulantiki] are discovered, "grafters in relation to the collective and state wealth, anti-Soviet gossips, etc.". And hence results the necessity of a further reinforcement of the dictatorship. In opposition to Engels, the workers' state must not "fall sleep", but on the contrary become more and more vigilant.

The picture drawn by the head of the Soviet government would be reassuring in the highest degree, were it not murderously self-contradictory. Socialism completely reigns in the country: "In that sense" classes are abolished. (If they are abolished in that sense, then they are in every other.) To be sure, the social harmony is broken here and there by fragments and remnants of the past, but it is impossible to think that scattered dreamers of a restoration of capitalism, deprived of power and property, together with "petty speculators" (not even *speculators*!) and "gossips" are capable of overthrowing the classless society. Everything is getting along, it seems, the very best you can imagine. But what is the use then of the iron dictatorship of the bureaucracy?

Those reactionary dreamers, we must believe, will gradually die out. The "petty speculators" and "gossips" might be disposed of with a laugh by the super-democratic Soviets. "We are not Utopians", responded Lenin in 1917 to the bourgeois and reformist theoreticians of the bureaucratic state, and "by no means deny the possibility and inevitability of excesses on the part of *individual persons,* and likewise the necessity for suppressing such excesses. But ... for this there is no need of a special machine, a special apparatus of repression. This will be done by the armed people themselves, with the same simplicity and ease with which any crowd of civilised people even in contemporary society separate a couple of fighters or stop an act of violence against a woman." These words sound as though the author has especially foreseen the remarks of his successors at the head of the government. Lenin is taught in the public schools of the Soviet Union, but apparently not in the Council of Peoples Commissars. Otherwise it would be impossible to explain Molotov's daring to resort without reflection to the very construction against which Lenin directed his well-sharpened weapons. The flagrant contradiction between the founder and his epigonies is before us! Whereas Lenin judged that even the liquidation of the exploiting classes might be accomplished without a bureaucratic apparatus, Molotov, in explaining why *after* the liquidation of classes the bureaucratic machine has strangled the independence of the people, find no better pretext than a reference to the "remnants" of the liquidated cases.

To live on these "remnants" becomes, however, rather difficult since, according to the confession of authoritative representatives of the bureaucracy itself, yesterday's class enemies are being successfully assimilated by the Soviet society. Thus Postyshev, one of the secretaries of the Central Committee of the party, said in April 1936 at a congress of the League of Youth: "Many of the sabotagers ... have sincerely repented and joined the ranks of the Soviet people." In view of the successful carrying out of collectivisation, "the children of Kulaks are not to be held responsible for their parents." And yet more: "The kulak himself now hardly believes in the possibility of a return to his former position of exploiter in the village." Not without reason did the government annul the limitations connected with social origin! But if Postyshev's assertion, wholly agreed to by Molotov, makes any sense it is only this: Not only has the bureaucracy become a monstrous anachronism, but the state compulsion in general has nothing whatever to do in the land of the Soviets. However, neither Molotov nor Postyshev agrees with that immutable inference. They prefer to hold the power even at the price of self-contradiction.

In reality, too, they cannot reject the power. Or, to translate this into objective language: The present Soviet Society cannot get along without a state, nor even – within limits – without a bureaucracy. But the cause of this is by no means the pitiful remnants of the past, but the mighty forces and tendencies of the present. The justification for the existence of the Soviet state as an apparatus of compulsion lies in the fact that the present transitional structure is still full of social contradictions, which in the sphere of *consumption* – most closely and sensitively felt by all – are extremely tense, and forever threaten to break over into the sphere of production. The triumph of socialism cannot be called either final or irrevocable.

The basis of bureaucratic rule is the poverty of society in objects of consumption, with the resulting struggle of each against all. Where there is enough goods in a store, the purchasers can come whenever they want to. When there is little goods, the purchasers are compelled to stand in line. When the lines are very long, it is necessary to appoint a policeman to keep order. Such is the starting point of the power of the Soviet bureaucracy. It "knows" who is to get something and who is to wait.

A raising of the material and cultural level ought, at first glance, to lessen the necessity of privileges, narrow the sphere of application of "bourgeois law", and thereby undermine the standing ground of its defenders, the bureaucracy. In reality the opposite thing has happened: the growth of the productive forces has been so far accompanied by an extreme development of all forms of inequality, privilege and advantage, and therewith of bureaucratism. This too is not accidental.

In its first period, the Soviet regime was undoubtedly far more equalitarian and less bureaucratic than now. But this was an equality of general poverty. The resources of the country were so scant that there was no opportunity to separate out from the masses of the population any broad privileged strata. At the same time the "equalising" character of wages, destroying personal interestedness, became a brake upon the development of the productive forces. Soviet economy had to lift itself from its poverty to a somewhat higher level before fat deposits of privilege became possible. The present state of production is still far from guaranteeing all necessities to everybody. But it is already adequate to give significant privileges to a minority, and convert inequality into a whip for the spurring on of the majority. That is the first reason why the growth of production has so far strengthened not the socialist, but the bourgeois features of the state.

But that is not the sole reason. Alongside the economic factor dictating capitalistic methods of payment at the present stage, there operates a parallel political factor in the person of the bureaucracy. In its very essence it is the planter and protector of inequality. It arose in the beginning as the bourgeois organ of the workers' state. In establishing and defending the advantages of a minority, it of course draws off the cream for its own use. Nobody who has wealth to distribute ever omits himself. Thus out of a social necessity there has developed an organ which has far outgrown its socially necessary function, and become an independent factor and therewith the source of great danger for the whole social organism.

The social meaning of the Soviet Thermidor now begins to take form before us. The poverty and cultural backwardness of the masses has again become incarnate in the malignant figure of the ruler with a great club in his hand. The deposed and abused bureaucracy, from being a servant of society, has again become its lord. On this road it has attained such a degree of social and moral alienation from the popular masses, that it cannot now permit any control over either its activities or its income.

The bureaucracy's seemingly mystic fear of "petty speculators, grafters, and gossips" thus finds a wholly natural explanation. Not yet able to satisfy the elementary needs of the population, the Soviet economy creates and resurrects at every step tendencies to graft and speculation. On the other side, the privileges of the new aristocracy awaken in the masses of the population a tendency to listen to anti-Soviet "gossips" – that is, to anyone who, albeit in a whisper, criticises the greedy and capricious bosses. It is a question, therefore, not of specters of the past, not of remnants of what no longer exists, not, in short, of the snows of yesteryear, but of new, mighty and continually reborn tendencies to personal accumulation. The first still very meagre wave of prosperity in the country, just because of its meagreness, has not weakened, but strengthened, these centrifugal tendencies, On the hand, there has developed simultaneously a desire of the underprivileged to slap the grasping hands of the new gentry. The social struggle again grows sharp. Such are the sources of the power of the bureaucracy. But from those same sources comes also a threat to its power.

-oOo-

Book Review

Architect of Bee, by Mike Cooley,
The Hogarth Press London
ISBN 0 7012 0769 8
Published 1987

As an individual, Mike Cooley was the epitome of a particular type. He came to prominence in Britain during the 1970's and 1980's, the period of decay of its old established system of capitalism, during which the irreconcilable conflicts between the classes were insistently manifesting themselves in ever new social forms. Inevitably, middle class individuals such as he reflect this class struggle and gravitate towards one side or the other. As a technician Cooley found his affinity with the working class.

These new forms, of course, were the result of the rapid developments in the technology of the means of production which resulted from micro technology of all kinds: All forms of computerisation such as robotics and CAD/CAM were violently transforming production processes and labour relations from which there was no escape for the working man. Cooley was a brilliant master of all these and a talented engineer in his own right. His great contribution was to grasp all this from the working man's perspective, help us to understand what was happening, and to create possibilities to resist their worst effects in the workplace and generally to our quality of life. We are reminded of the old saying – if Cooley had not existed it would have been necessary to invent him.

The working class, spontaneously driven by the historical need to socialise the means of production and distribution, was reaching out blindly for practical control over the industrial system into which they were obliged to liquidate their lives and those of their families. The old revolutionary idea of workers' control swam out from the depts of a sea of factory closures, redundancies, new and ever more exploitative employment relations. But as we shall see, Cooley's interpretation of this working class demand for control over the production process robbed it of its revolutionary socialistic content and delivered it into the hands of the employers as a weapon directed against the very class whose interests he championed.

These two conceptualisations of the industrial process, new technology and workers control, are organically, that is dialectically, inseparable, each mediating the other. How does Cooley understand them?

Not without logical justification, he sees the introduction of new technology as an opportunity to extend workers' control over their working conditions, but unfortunately the revolutionary relation between these is utterly lost on him, and with that loss came the incapacity to understand the nature of either as taken in themselves.

New technology is a means of increasing the productivity of labour, but such progress can serve two conflicting purposes. On the one hand it can serve a step towards socialist society which must of necessity rest on higher levels of productivity than capitalism can achieve, and on the other it can serve as a means to prolong the agonising exploitation of labour by capital. This we have known at least since the publication of the first volume of *Capital* by Karl Marx in 1867.

"But machinery not only acts as a competitor who gets the better of the working man, and is constantly on the point of making him superfluous. It is also a power inimical to him, and as such capital proclaims it from the roof-tops and as such makes use of it. It is the most powerful weapon for repressing strikes, those periodic revolts of the working class against the autocracy of capital. According to Gaskell, the steam engine was from the very start an antagonist of human power, an antagonist that enabled the capitalist to tread under foot the growing claims of the workmen, who threatened the newly born factory system with a crisis. It would be possible to write quite a history of the inventions, made since 1830, **for the sole purpose of supplying capital with weapons against the revolt of the working class.**" (Karl Marx, *Capital Vol.1*, page 435. My emphasis.)

And further down the same page:

"Ure says of a machine used in calico printing: 'at length capitalists sought deliverance from this intolerable bondage' [namely the, in their eyes, burdensome terms of their contracts with the workmen] 'in the resources of science, and were speedily re-instated in their legitimate rule, that of the head over the inferior members'"

Here we see the introduction of new technology, indeed deeper still even science itself, in its true social relation, the prime means of the enslavement of the working class by capital *as its very purpose,* and in this respect there is not the slightest difference between the steam engine and the newest micro-technology. Marx continues to quote Ure:

" 'Then the combined malcontents, who fancied themselves impregnably intrenched behind the old lines of division of labour, found their flanks turned and their defences rendered useless by the new **mechanical tactics**, and were obliged to surrender at discretion.' With regard to the invention of the self-acting mule, he says: 'A creation destined to restore order among the industrious classes ... This invention confirms the great doctrine already propounded, that when capital enlists science her service, the refractory hand of labour will always be taught docility.'" (*Ibid.* My emphasis)

And so, we see, the use of new technology as an infinitely present means of enslaving the working class was long ago *consciously* raised to "a great doctrine" of bourgeois social science. In any case, for so long as capitalism endures new technology will never increase the productivity of labour beyond the limits of the individual enterprise, since the measure of labour productivity as an economic parameter must be amortised over the *whole* working population, including the ever increasing army of unemployed whom the capitalists sacked … wait for it … in order to raise the productivity of labour! In practice, Cooley unintentionally served this cause.

It is a pity that Cooley, who appeals to Marx for a title of his book, did not read Volume One of *Capital* with greater attention. Had he done so he would have written a different book. "Marx did not leave us a logic", Engels has remarked, "but he did leave us the logic of *Capital*". Cooley was blind to it. Instead of Marx's method of dialectical materialism we get a cognitive method set out in sophisticated graphical forms according to the logic of simple arithmetic. From the political point of view, in particular with respect to the class struggle, there is nothing further to be said about it.

His book, as a result, is based on the method of metaphysical eclecticism carried to extraordinary complexity and a deep and sympathetic understanding of the human cost of the brutal imposition of this new technology in the workplace and beyond, and this in itself is not without revolutionary significance. He held up a mirror, so to speak, for the workers to see themselves and understand their dilemma. He writes:

"Above all this, there is a seething unhappiness among both manual and intellectual workers because the resultant systems tend to absorb their knowledge from them, and render them abject appendages to the machines and systems being developed. Those who are not directly involved in using the equipment are merely confused bystanders. I find a deep concern that individuals feel frustrated because their common sense and knowledge, and their practical experience, whether as a skilled worker, a designer, a mother, a father, a teacher or a nurse, are less and less relevant and are almost an impediment to 'progress'." (Page10)

Here we see what is new and highly significant. We have grown used to manual skills being absorbed into new machinery, but now mental capacities and actual knowledge, our very thoughts, are being taken from us in order to render us surplus to the labour process. This process, of course, was painful and damaging most of all for those who had spent years at study and had no doubts about their creative worth. Heart attacks and mental breakdowns became commonplace among technicians and management. Many retired early, taking their priceless talents with them. But for all his understanding of this crisis in the world of manufacture Cooley seems to have no grasp of its wider social implications. Frequently we see such formulations as this:

"Hopefully we can examine the nature of this 'progress' and seek to identify alternatives which would constitute real progress and involve masses of ordinary people in the definition and construction of that progress." (*Ibid.*)

Either Cooley learned nothing from his reading of Marx, or he is afraid to say it out loud. In the first place, "people" is an abstraction; people are either workers or capitalists, and the crisis in industry gives rise to the irreconcilable conflict between these two classes. What is the "real progress" and what would be its transforming Essence? Resolution of the class contradictions peacefully under capitalism? Revolutionary overthrow of the capitalist state and the imposition of workers state control under the dictatorship of the proletariat?

The title of Chapter Six, (page 87), brings us to the crucial question, *Political Implications of New Technology*. For the Marxist, such implications immediately pose the necessity for social revolution, but Cooley is firstly concerned with the "male/female values" rather than the class struggle. As we have quoted above, the purpose of the introduction of new technology is to enslave the working class, but at the same time it increases productivity towards the level required for socialist property relations and planned production.

Cooley is mostly remembered for his practical attempt to solve this problem by advancing the *Corporate Plan* for Lucas Aerospace, a Utopian attempt to divert capitalist production for profit into production for social need. His idea was meant to address four perceived contradictions in the productive process:

The difference between what technology can provide for society and what it actually provides.

Waste of the talent and enthusiasm of the workforce which results in unemployment.

The myth of new technology – the suggestion that it benefits the worker in the workplace.

Hostility of society to new technology as it is practiced.

(See page 114)

All of these, of course, express the burning need for social revolution, but the idea that such problems can be addressed any other way is naïve Utopianism. He submitted his plan to 180 institutions including universities, trade unions and other authorities and was surprised that he got absolutely no response. Undaunted Cooley continued to struggle with other ideas, and to be sure he uncovered much truth and advanced our understanding of these burning issues, but to no avail. To this day there are those who try to continue the initiative without success,

He seeks to penetrate below the relations of production to more fundamental social questions. Pointing out that scientific progress has become and ideological support for bourgeois society, "the outgoing social order", he writes:

"There is now a growing realisation that science has embodied within it many of the ideological assumptions of the society which has given rise to it. This in turn has resulted in a questioning of the neutrality of science as at present practiced in our society. The debate on this issue is likely to be one of major political significance. The question extends so far beyond that of scientific abuses, to the deeper considerations of the nature of the scientific process itself. Science done within a particular social order reflects the norms and ideology of that social order. Science ceases to be seen as autonomous, but instead as part of an interacting system in which the internalised ideological assumptions help to determine the very experimental designs and theories of scientists themselves." (Page 90)

Here is deep penetration of the social issues posed by the production process in a class divided society. Certainly scientific thought and practice *cannot* be neutral; the dominant ideology of a class divided society is that of the politically ruling class. But still the Marxist understanding goes deeper. The production of scientific values, including scientific ideas, ("intellectual property rights"), are like everything else, determined by the universal production relations in a given society, and in capitalist society that means commodity production and exchange. The production system does indeed reflect the dominant ideology, but it does more than that, it *reproduces that ideology itself.* Since *this* commodity must necessarily be exchanged, then *all* commodities must be exchanged. Every time a worker produces a commodity he reproduces bourgeois relations of production and distribution along with it, and along with this objective development comes the subjective, the perpetuation of bourgeois subjective individualism. "All that is rational is real", says Hegel. This is the secret of the ideological enslavement of labour by capital.

Cooley continues to penetrate the question:

"It will therefore be necessary to change the nature of the ownership of the means of production, although this in itself will by no means be adequate. In addition there is the question as the whether there is a contradiction (non-antagonistic) between science and technology in their present form and the very essence of humanity. It is quite conceivable that our scientific methodology, in particular our design methodology, has been distorted by the social forces that have given rise to it. The question is therefore whether the problems of scientific development and technological change, which are primarily due to the nature of or class-divided society, can be solved solely by changing the economic base of that society." (Page 108)

Well, he has already pointed out that the form of society affects, shapes, the productive process, and it is now self-evident that monumental changes in actual production, both quantitative and qualitative, are a prerequisite to the survival of organic life on Earth. The key questions here are "changing the nature of the ownership of the means of production" and "the economic base of society". How must this be done?

"The question is not one of mere theoretical and academic interest. It must be the burning issue in the minds of those attempting to build a peoples democracy." (*Ibid.*)

Since Cooley is fond of invoking the wisdom of Marx, (without ever giving exact references), it is necessary to place clear blue water between his view and the Marxist view of the crucial question he has posed. There is a vital qualitative difference – the age-old difference between the Utopian theory of socialism, and the Marxist, scientific theory. His concept of a "peoples' democracy" as the basis of socialised means of production is clearly of the Utopian kind, and Engels dismissed that long ago:

"Then came the three great Utopians; Saint-Simon, to whom the middle class movement, side by side with the proletarian, still had a certain significance; Fourier; and Owen, who in the country where capitalist production was most developed, and under the influence of the antagonisms begotten of this, worked out his proposals for the removal of class distinction systematically and in direct relation to French materialism.

"One thing is common to all three. None of them appears as a representative of the interests of that proletariat which historical development had, in the meantime, produced. Like the French philosophers, they do not claim to emancipate a particular class to begin with, but all humanity at once. Like them, they wish to bring in the kingdom of reason and eternal justice, but this kingdom, as they see it, is as far as heaven from earth, from that of the French philosophers." (*Socialism: Utopian and Scientific*. This pamphlet length article appears in various publications)

The difference between the Utopian and scientific, Marxist conception of socialism, it that the Utopian socialism does not understand the history of human society as the history of the struggle between classes, does not understand the class struggle in the present, and therefore does not understand that the idea of a "peoples democracy" is an impossibility, that the progress which Cooley seeks can only unfold as a *working class* democracy, in contra-distinction to the bourgeois, (capitalist), democracy under which we now live and which is threatening to put an end to human habitation of this planet.

Cooley's grasp of the technical and scientific aspects of the production process under decaying capitalism was encyclopaedic and creative, but he never transcended the limits of the bourgeois ideology upon which it rests and which it constantly reproduces. It is frustrating to think what a decisive contribution he might have made to the social revolution under the guidance of Marxist revolutionary leadership

-oOo-

Our National Freedom

Discussion document shortly following the general election of December 2019

Struggles of all kinds advance and retreat. The Thatcher/Blair conspiracy were years of retreat for the working class. Then came a spontaneous upsurge from the depths of the working class which took the Labour leaders by surprise and Corbyn was thrust into the leadership of the Labour Party in 2015. He is doing his job superbly under a hail of fire but it is only a matter of time before the right wing who control the party machine oust Corbyn. This was the situation in the Labour Party for the election.

The issue which divided the country and determined the outcome of the election was "Brexit", Britain's exit from the European Union. Labour campaigned on class issues, NHS, employment, social security. "for the many not the few". But the Tories focused on "Brexit" and this secured their return with a big majority.

Now we must understand what is being done to us by the ruling class – we are being torn away from Europe in preparation for direct rule by the USA, hence Major's and Heseltine's appeal during the election process, "put your country first and don't vote Tory". This from a one-time Tory Prime Minister and a cabinet minister.)

US president Trump has begun final preparations to change the political landscape of Britain to fit direct rule from the USA. He has spoken to the Queen twice, no doubt to inform her that she is not part of his plan, his intention being to install a presidential system with dictatorial powers, and he has instructed Farrage (a far-right leader) to campaign for the abolition of the House of Lords. He has subverted the democratic Parliamentary election process by means a total monopoly of all media outlets and possibly other means unknown to us. After the subversion of the 2017 referendum on EU membership and now this we can conclude that bourgeois democracy is at an end in Britain. His fascist blood-hound, Steve Bannon, has explained in an interview that "we are going to change Britain … if you want to change a thing you first have to smash it … the British people do not know the turmoil that is coming to them …". Follow this link … https://www.bbc.co.uk/news/av/world-us-canada-49169829/steve-bannon-the-brexit-turmoil-is-only-just-beginning.

The historical background is as follows:

World War II brought an effective end to the era of imperialism and began the process of uniting all the advanced capitalist countries into the system of Global Capitalism. The two great antagonists in the struggle for empire, Britain defending hers and Germany trying to establish one, fought each other to a standstill. The only winner was the USA, but her method of world domination was not the old imperialist way, but rather to rule through direct economic dictatorship, the almighty dollar. On average other countries' dollar imports are worth five times what they buy from America. Over half of world debt is in dollars and dollars make up two-thirds of central-bank reserves. This system, which operates through the hegemony of the international banking system, The World Bank, the IMF, *etcetera*, has in recent years become a directly political and military force.

This is the cause of all the wars. Whereas under the old imperialist system the mother county constructed its own state machine, government system, education, police, civil service etc, in the colonies, now puppet systems are installed by force. The classic case was Iraq. America was happy enough with Saddam till he started to trade oil in Euros. Then they had to stop him by military invasion to protect the dollar. It is the same situation, one way or another, with all the wars the USA fights. The struggle now is between China and the USA for supremacy under global capitalism

Now we, in Britain, have become the victims of this global conflict. Having become enslaved to American banks and its markets the British capitalist class must now bow to its political rule. This process began with the Thatcher/Blair conspiracy whose purpose was firstly to hijack the Labour Party and to transform it into just another liberal (with a small letter l) party, thus robbing the working class of its political leadership and reducing us to a de-classed, disunited mass of individuals. All seemed to be going well for them till they tried to put the final touch to their plan, the election of the Party leader by one-man-one vote; then in 2015 it all blew up in the faces.

We shall never forget the genuine shock and amazement on Blairs face. Bewildered, he could only stammer, "I am shocked and appalled at the election of Jeremy Corbyn." Clearly this man had never given a thought to the nature of the British working class. The first such class in history, united in its own organisations even so far back as the Levellers, Chartists, and firmly founded trade unions, and finally the Labour Party, it is an historically established social substance comprising the vast working class mass of the nation, a class which can ultimately never be defeated. We know this because the check given to their plan to destroy the Labour Party did not come from the leadership; it came from below in the form of a spontaneous mass uprising of the conscious layer of the working class - hundreds of thousands joined the Party to vote for Corbyn.

Corbyn understood the situation "It's not me they are afraid of", he kept saying, "it's you", pointing at the thousands of people who flocked to his meetings, and he coined the political demand, "for the many not the few". This latter perfectly expresses the essence of this important historical moment; the masses had risen up in defiance of the Thatcher/Blair attack.

Now, with the return of the Tories in the 2019 General Election, the American leaders of global capitalism have counter-attacked by subverting the British democratic system. The British people did not vote for Boris Johnson, the US president Trump appointed him. Their main and only weapon was the appalling lie in a plethora of forms, pumped out 24/7 through their vast propaganda machine. Let us not forget that every newspaper, radio and TV channel is their property and it did their bidding enthusiastically. These lies plumbed such disgusting depths as to come as a shock to even the most cynical working class activist. The true significance of all this is that it indicates the depth of the historical bankruptcy of the global capitalist class. A class which can only continue its existence by falsehood is destined for the dustbin of history. The working class, however, is the revolutionary class and the future is ours. Our perspective must be to struggle to free ourselves from the rule of the United States and at the same time to work for international unity of the working class in the struggle for social transformation

What now for the working class and its political leadership, the Labour Party? Left reformism has found some new ground in the Party. The so-called "parachuting-in" of new candidates who are young and committed to the Corbyn orientation – "for the many not the view", will fight on this ground, and the conscious layers of the working class have been educated and motivated to some degree. But, we may be sure, the right wing reaction will win back much of this ground, and in any case the road to the emancipation of the working class does not pass through Parliamentary reformism. For that Marxist revolutionary leadership is necessary.

Terry Button
December 2019

The Moscow Trials
The Greatest Injustice in History

During the 1930's a series of court trials took place in the Soviet Union. The indictment against those accused was that they had conspired as a group with foreign powers, notably Nazi Germany, to assassinate Stalin and other Soviet leaders, overthrow the Soviet socialist system by terrorist methods and restore capitalism.

The strange thing was that all of the accused had been Bolsheviks, close associates of Lenin and leaders of the revolution. Why, having dedicated their lives to the struggle for revolution and socialism, making courageous sacrifices in their cause, should they suddenly wish to destroy all they had achieved? This contradiction has been observed in connection with every revolution in history and can only be understood against the background of the history of the Russian Revolution itself. Trotsky explained as follows:

"It is sufficiently well known that every revolution up to this time has been followed by a reaction, or even a counter revolution. This, to be sure, has never thrown the nation all the way back to its starting point, but it has always taken from the people the lion's share of their conquests. The victim of the first reactionary wave have been, as a general rule, those pioneers, initiators, and instigators who stood at the head of the masses in the period of the revolutionary offensive. In their stead stood people of the second line, in league with the former enemies of the revolution, have been advance to the front. Beneath this dramatic duel of 'coryphées' on the open political scene, shifts have taken place in the relations between the classes and, no less important, profound changes in the psychology of the recently revolutionary masses.

"Answering the bewildered questions of many comrades as to what has become of the activity of the Bolshevik Party and the working class – where is its revolutionary initiative, its spirit of self-sacrifice and plebeian pride – why, in place of all this, has appeared so much vileness, cowardice, pusillanimity and careerism – Rakovsky referred to the life story of the French Revolution of the eighteenth century, and offered the example of Bebeuf, who on emerging from the Abbaye prison likewise wondered what had become of the heroic people of the Parisian suburbs. A revolution is a mighty devourer of human energy, both individual and collective. The nerves give way. Consciousness is shaken and characters worn out. Events unfold too swiftly for the flow of fresh forces to replace the loss. Hunger, unemployment, the death of the revolutionary cadres, the removal of the masses from administration, all this led to such a physical and moral impoverishment of the Parisian suburbs that they required three decades before they were ready for a new insurrection." (L. Trotsky, *Revolution Betrayed*, New Park Publications, page 88)

Trotsky wrote this in 1936 just before the first trial, and he knew it well from personal experience, since by this time he had been ousted from all his leading government positions, expelled from the Bolshevik Party (now renamed the Communist Party), deprived of Soviet citizenship and sent into exile. So the explanation to the question above, why did the leaders of the Revolution renounce all they had fought for and plot to overthrow is it simple – they did not. The accusations against them were entirely false and the evidence was fabricated by the counter-revolutionary opponents of the Revolution, the "people of the second line" who had now risen to positions of power and subverted the revolution in the interests of the now overthrown ruling class. These were, firstly, the Mensheviks, the social democrats who had opposed the Revolution and organised the "White" armies under Czarist leaders such as Admiral Kolchak and General Deniken, which started civil the war to overthrow the Revolution in 1918. They were financed by capitalist countries such as Britain, France and Germany which sent in their own armies. Such was the scale of their betrayal.

How did they conduct their persecution against the revolutionary leaders at the trials?

The chief state prosecutor was Andrei Vyshinsky, a Menshevik who had previously held a similar position under the repressive Czarist regime. He was opposed to the revolution from the start and had once signed an order to have Lenin arrested. His presentation of the case was characterised from the start by personal anger and hatred of the accused, full of inuendo and moral condemnation, none of which would be accepted in any properly conducted legal proceeding. The evidence consisted almost entirely of confessions that had been extracted from the accused under prolonged imprisonment and torture and were obviously false. In his pamphlet, *Behind the Moscow Trial*, the American Trotskyist Max Shachtman, who led a thorough review of the first trial, quotes from the indictment as follows:

"The 'newly revealed circumstances establish beyond doubt', reads the indictment, 'that at the end of 1932 the Trotskyist Zinoviev groups united and formed a united centre consisting of Zinoviev, Kamenev, Yevdokimov, Bakayev (from the Zinovievists) and I.N. Smirnov. Ter-Vaganian and Mrachkovsky (from the Trotskyists). The principle condition for the union of these counter-revolutionary groups was their common recognition of individual terrorism against the leaders of the CPSU (b) and the Soviet Government (1589f).'" (Page 16. The

CPSU(b) is the Communist Party of the Soviet Union - Bolshevik.)

And in his concluding speech before the Tribunal, prosecutor Vyshinsky declared:

"I consider it absolutely proved by the personal testimony of literally all concerned, including on this score that of Smirnov, that this centre was organised on a terrorist basis, that the centre worked with terroristic methods and did not shrink from the most sordid and cynical fighting methods." (*Ibid.*)

Here it must be firmly understood that all through the revolutionary struggle of these Bolsheviks under Lenin's leadership terroristic methods were understood to be totally counter-productive and firmly ruled out. Shachtman continues:

"Let us see if the 'personal testimony of literally all the accused' proves any such thing. In reading, remember that all these men are on trial for their lives; that, therefore, the very least the prosecutor (and a Soviet prosecutor at that!) owes the accused, if nobody else, is a scrupulous verification of every single assertion, a checking and re-checking of dates and places and individuals, until there was no doubt left in anybody's mind that the charges were true.

"At the very outset, therefore, the fact must be recorded that not one single piece of evidence was introduced at the trial – not a single document, not a single letter, not a scrap of paper - to prove the existence of the conspiracy that allegedly lasted for four years and directly involved scores of men and women in at least five countries. The prosecution claims the original existence of any number of documents, and if half or even less than half of them were produced in court, they might have proved the charges with infinitely more conviction than the mutually conspiritory testimony of the 16 defendants and the two 'witnesses' (Yakovlev and Safonova), both of whom are on trial for their lives in other cases."

Nor was the verbal evidence of the accused, taken as a whole, any serious indication of guilt. Each defendant gave conflicting evidence concerning relevant facts and there were four different dates given for the beginning of the conspiracy. Clearly the evidence had been extracted under torture and was completely false and the whole trial was an incredibly clumsy construction from beginning to end. So how did the world at large, the press and legal profession, in the west, and most particularly the Communist Party of Great Britain, receive the news and report it?

"The first of the three great trials took place in August 1936. Immediately upon publication of the indictment, the 'DW', [*Daily Worker*, newspaper of the Communist Party of Great Britain, TB] came out with an editorial (August 17) accepting the guilt of the accused men. 'These revelations ... will fill all decent people with loathing and hatred ... Crowning infamy of all is the evidence showing how they were linked up with the Nazi Secret Police ...' This instantaneous and whole-hearted endorsement of whatever Stalin's policemen chose to allege at any given moment was to prove characteristic of the British Stalinist reactions to each successive trial." (*The Moscow Trials Anthology*, New Park Publications, 1967)

A further editorial, on 22 August, demonstrated a feature common to all Stalinist publications in all countries – this arrogant habit of telling their readers what to think, and telling them what everyone else thinks without taking any steps to find out:

> " 'The extent and organisation of the plot, with its cold blooded killings of the leaders of the working class, has shocked the Labour and Socialist movement of the world.' At this point of course no "cold blooded killings" had taken place at all, and the real effect of the trial was to compromise the Soviet Union in the eyes of many workers and to play into the hands of the most right-wing sections." (*Ibid.*)

Indeed, it was these disgusting trials, aimed directly at the real leaders of the revolution, upon which the Trotskyist movement gained decisive advances at the expense of the Stalinists. Important sections of the CPGB and its supporters deserted them in significant numbers and joined the Trotskyists. However, the most telling thing was the response of the ruling class and its press.

> " 'On the other hand, any expression of approval for the trial by a bourgeois newspaper or other source was to be eagerly seized upon and publicised during these years, and already in this issue we find *The Observer* quoted in a special box, as saying: *It is futile the think the trial was staged and the charges trumped up*'" (*Ibid.*)

Here we see the class nature of the trials – to the satisfaction of the Stalinists they served the capitalist class and the counter-revolution. It was the same in every country and the campaign of lies and slander took on a life of its own, spilling beyond the limits of the trial itself to become a general attack on the leaders of the revolution. Every Stalinist hack and sympathiser jumped on the bandwagon. In the *Daily Worker* on August 28 one Ralph Fox attacked the main accused, Trotsky himself, with an article quaintly titled *Trotsky was no Great General*. He Should have been aware of the views expressed by his master Stalin before the counter-revolutionary reaction set in and the truth was recent public knowledge which even the insanely jealous Stalin was forced to acknowledge.

"The bureaucratic revision of the history of the Party and the revolution is taking place under Stalin's direct supervision. The sign-posts of the work clearly mark off the stages of the development of the Soviet machine. On the 6th. November 1918 (new style) Stalin wrote in an anniversary article in Pravda.

"The inspirer of the revolution from beginning to end was the Central Committee of the Party headed by Comrade Lenin. Vladimir Ilych was then living in Petrograd in a conspiritative apartment in the Vyborg district. On the evening of October 24 he was summoned to Smolny for the general leadership of the movement. All the work of the practical organisation of the insurrection was conducted under the immediate leadership of the president of the Petrograd Soviet, Comrade Trotsky. It is possible to declare with certainty that the swift passing of the garrison to the side of the Soviet, and the skilful direction of the work of the Military Revolutionary Committee, the Party owes principally and first of all to Comrade Trotsky. Comrades Antonov and Podvoisky were Comrade Trotsky's chief assistants." (L. Trotsky, *History of the Russian Revolution*, Vol.3, page 343)

As for Trotsky's generalship, the facts are quite different. Trotsky was appointed Commissar for War by the Central

Committee of which Stalin was a member, and went on the build the Red Army and lead it to victory in the civil war. Lenin, we know, had complete confidence in Trotsky and gave him all the support he could. At the height of the civil war he provided Trotsky with blank documents for written military orders with his signature attached:

"Comrades: Knowing the strict character of Comrade Trotsky's orders, I am so convinced, so absolutely convinced, of the correctness, expediency, and necessity for the success of the cause of the order given by Comrade Trotsky, that I unreservedly endorse this order. V. Ulyanov/Lenin" (*The Case of Leon Trotsky*, page 72)

The second trial began in January 1937. There were 17 accused, all leaders of the revolution, including Pyatakov, Radek, Sokolnikov, Muralov and Serebryakov. The charges were the same as for the first trial and all were shot. Behind the scenes a secret trial of the military leadership took place and the highest leaders, including the talented Tukhachevsky, were all shot. It was a secret trial and there were no confessions, possibly because soldiers are made of sterner stuff and they withstood the torture. On 12 June the Daily Worker reported this trial as follows:

" … thanks to the unrelaxing vigilance of the Soviet intelligence service, a further shattering blow has been given to the criminal war-making elements who seek to undermine and destroy the Socialist Father-land of the international working class."

On 14 June a *Daily Worker* announcement said "Red Army Traitors Executed" and informed us that "the workers of Britain will rejoice". On 16 June The Central Committee of the CPGB issued a statement congratulating the Soviet

Government on the executions and welcomed, on behalf of the British workers, "the wiping out of the bureaucratic degenerates associated with fascism." Every leading member of the CPSU placed his or her self on record supporting the repressions - and we are bound to ask – who gave these class traitors the right to speak on behalf of the British workers?

On 16 June 1937 their Central Committee passed the following resolution on the trials and military purges:

"The Communist Party of Great Britain congratulates the workers and peasants of the Soviet Union, their Party and their government on the drastic measures which they are taking to root out wreckers and spies from their midst ... it is a sign of healthy vigilance on the part of the workers of the USSR that ... they are dealing with wreckers and spies under the influence of Trotsky ... The works of great Britain ... will welcome the wiping out of the bureaucratic degeneration associated with fascism ..." (Quoted in *Stalinism in Britain*, Robert Black, page108)

The CPGB have never, to this day, repudiated this appalling sycophantic nonsense. The newspaper associated with the Labour Party, the *Daily Herald,* expressed "deep concern" at the response of the CPGB to this situation, The General Secretary, John Gollan, replied on 1 July as follows:

"The *Daily Herald* is deeply concerned about the Communist Party's attitude with regard to the situation in the Soviet Union. Why have we not spoken out about the 'terrible wave of executions', the astonishing extermination of leading communist citizens of the Soviet Union, 'the firing squads that kill Stalin's opponents'? ... *The reason the Communists have not dealt with these events is that they have not taken place.* Eight generals have been shot, 40 pro-fascists wreckers have been executed in Siberia, leading Communists who have neglected their public duty have been removed from their posts, but to magnify these events into 'terrible waves of executions and arrests, vast and astonishing extermination' is to be guilty of *Daily Mail* hysteria, (Our emphasis)" (*Ibid.*)

Clearly, these crimes to which Gollan admits amount to a "terrible wave" as they are and need no magnification to appal any right-thinking person, and we know that this was just the tip of the iceberg. But it wasn't just the Stalinists who approved of these crimes; most tellingly it was their masters in the bourgeois class. D.N. Pritt, a KC and Labour Party politician, went to the Soviet Union in 1932 on behalf of the New Fabian Research Bureau to find the facts. In the *Report of the Court Proceedings, Case of the Trotskyite-Zinovievite Terrorist Centre* which was published in 1936, the English translation from the Russian, he wrote:

"Once again the more faint-hearted socialists are beset with doubts and anxieties ... but once again we can feel confident that when the smoke has rolled away from the battlefield of controversy it will be realised that the charge was true, the confessions correct, and the prosecution fairly conducted ..." (*The Moscow Trials Anthology*, New Park, page 3)

This from a senior British "King's Council"

Finally the fourth trial began in March 1938. The chief accused was Trotsky himself and the whole of Lenin's Politbureau was included. Again the same charges, the same forced and conflicting confessions and the same sentence.

However, we do not need to confine ourselves to the conduct of the trials to ascertain their Nature. Their truth has been fully revealed more recently, particularly after the death of Stalin in 1953. At the 20th congress of the CPSU in 1956 Khrushchev revealed it all in his famous "secret speech".

"We have to consider seriously and analyse correctly the crimes of the Stalin era in order that we may preclude any possibility of a repetition in any form whatever of what took place during the life of Stalin, who absolutely did not tolerate collegiality in leadership and in work, and who practiced brutal violence, not only toward everything which was opposed to him, but also toward that which seemed to his capricious and despotic character, contrary to his concepts."

And here is the most telling part of his speech:

"It was determined [on investigation] that of 139 members and candidates of the Party's Central Committee who were elected at the 17th. 1934] Congress, 98 persons. i.e. 70%, were arrested and shot (mostly in 1937 and 1938). What was the composition of the delegates to the 17th. Congress? It is known that 80% of the voting participants of the 17th. Congress joined the Party during the years of conspiracy before the Revolution and during the civil war; this means before 1921. By social origin the basic mass of delegates to the congress were workers (60% of the voting members). For this reason, it was inconceivable that a congress so composed would have elected a Central Committee a majority of whom would prove to be enemies of the Party. The only reason why 70% of the Central Committee members and candidates elected at the 17th. Congress were branded as enemies of the Party and the people was because honest Communists were slandered, accusations against them were fabricated, and revolutionary legality was gravely undermined. The same fate met not only the Central Committee members but also the majority of the delegates to the 17th. Congress. Of 1,966 delegates with either voting or advisory rights, 1,108 persons were arrested on charges of anti-revolutionary crimes ..."

Nearly all these leaders were later accused of having been in league with imperialism since 1918 and shot. Before our eyes, before history, the Communist leaders of the Russian Revolution were massacred ... by Stalin. Thus we are informed as to the social composition of the early Soviet leaders who attended the 17th. Congress and who, along with many of similar background but who were not delegates to the Congress, were murdered on Stalin's orders. Clearly Stalin's political power base was not the working class and the Revolution, so what was it? We shall have to seek the answer from a different source since Khrushchev did not provide it in his speech:

"It would be naïve to imagine that Stalin, previously unknown to the masses, suddenly issued from the wings full armed with a complete strategical plan. No indeed. Before he felt out his own course, the bureaucracy felt out Stalin himself. He brought it all the necessary guarantees: the prestige of an old Bolshevik, a strong character, narrow vision, and close bonds with the political machine as the sole source of his influence. The success which fell upon him was a surprise at first to Stalin himself. It was the friendly welcome of the new ruling group, trying to free itself from the old principles and from the control of the masses, and having need of a reliable arbiter in its inner affairs. A secondary figure before the masses and in the events of the revolution, Stalin revealed himself as the indubitable leader of the Thermidorian bureaucracy, as first in its midst." (*Revolution Betrayed,* page 92-93, L. Trotsky).

What was the social composition of the bureaucratic clique who had appointed Stalin their leader? Trotsky goes on:-

"The new ruling caste soon revealed its own ideas, feeling and, more important, its interests. The overwhelming majority of the older generation of the present bureaucracy had stood on the other side of the barricades during the October Revolution. (Take, for example, Troyanovsky, Maisky, Potemkin, Suritz, Khinchuk, etc.) Or at best they had stood aside from the struggle. Those of the present bureaucrats who were in the Bolshevik camp in the October days played in the majority of cases no considerable role. As for the young bureaucrats, they have been chosen and educated by the elders, frequently from among their own offspring. These people could not have achieved the October Revolution, but they were perfectly suited to exploit it." (*Ibid.*)

Clearly the massacre of the communist representatives of the *revolutionary* working class was carried out by bourgeois, non-communist social strata and was thoroughly *counter-revolutionary*, but Khrushchev could not possibly have gone so far as to explain all this in his speech. Indeed, it seems likely that his motivation was self-preservation as much as anything else. Another Soviet leader, Anastas Mikoyan, later claimed to have suggested the idea to Khrushchev, saying "There has to be a report on what had happened ... if we don't do that at the Congress, and someone else does it some time before the next congress, then everyone would have a legal right to hold us fully responsible for the crimes that had occurred".

So the rats were trying to save their own skins. Finally we must remark, that the only Soviet Citizen who colluded with the Nazis was Stalin himself, since he entered into a pact with them in 1940 and conspired with them to jointly invade Poland. Such was the cynicism of the man and the counter-revolutionary conspiracy he led. The Communist Party of the Soviet Union disbanded in 1991 following the disempowerment of the Kremlin dictatorship under Gorbachev's reforms, and the CPGB, unable to survive for one day without is Stalinist mentors, did the same. Its last acts were to defend the Stalinists when they sent in the tanks to crush the workers revolution in Hungary in 1956 and in Czechoslovakia in 1974. Since then a new party, The Communist Party of Britain, has been formed, but neither party ever repudiated its murderous counter-revolutionary nature and admitted to its crimes against the working class.

-oOo-

Letter to John Gollan

Here we reproduce a letter from Gerry Healy, a leader of the British Trotskyist movement, to a leader of the British Stalinists. It is clear that, even as late as 1967, the Stalinists were still upholding the lies of the murderous Kremlin dictatorship. In this way they serve only the interests of counter-revolutionary ruling class by bringing the communist movement into disrepute in the eyes of the workers. No reply to this letter was ever received. (TB)

John Gollan
Secretary, British Communist Party
16 King Street
Covent Garden
London, W. C. 2
14th November, 1967

You have recently returned from the Soviet Union where you were present with Stalin's old comrades-in-arms celebrating the 50th Anniversary of the October Revolution.

How is it possible for you, on behalf of the British Communist Party, to celebrate such an event when you still condone the frame-up and murder by Stalin in the Moscow Trials of the 1930's of the overwhelming majority of the men who led the Revolution of 1917?

Your colleague Mr. James Klugman, interviewed in the BBC's "Woman's Hour" on Thursday December 1, 1966, made the following condemnation of these trials:

Klugman: I've travelled and watched people being killed, driven underground, ah … I've been looked at and laughed at at times. I've known defeats as well as victories, and of course I've questioned. I've seen people in the name of Communism do things that are not Communist and are bad and ugly. And I've been ashamed of them.

Interviewer: Such as?

Klugman: such as for instance the trials in Russia, in …in… in the 30's which I came to see were wrong and ugly.

Mr. Klugman is the Educational Director of your Party and a member of its Executive Committee. Do you agree with what he said on the BBC?

You and other leaders of the Communist Party, such as Ramelson, Palme Dutt, J. R. Campbell and Rothstein, know full well that Stalin was nothing more than a brutal murderer of Bolshevik leaders. We note the Klugman, who says one thing on the BBC, similarly remains silent, as you remained silent when it came to the 50th Anniversary.

Obviously there are people in your leadership who keep their private thoughts to themselves on these murders, whilst you, as the public figure, go on supporting Stalin's crimes against the international working class, knowing that it is these very crimes that are responsible for the contempt which tens of thousands of people have for the British Communist Party.

Not a single lesson can be learned from the October Revolution without these enormous wrongs being put right, but this is far from what the present leadership in the Soviet Union wish you to do. Yet again, they have produced another history book which is just a falsified as those which were produced in the past, and here again you prefer to remain silent.

You also remain silent when you know that the Stalinist agent who murdered Trotsky is reported today to be residing in Czechoslovakia.

You will not be allowed to get away with this contemptible support for murderers. Those of us who have fought for Marxism in Britain against Stalinism will hold you responsible for what happened in the Moscow Trials in the '30s. You supported these crimes then because you were Stalin's man, and you support them now because you are still Stalin's man. The only difference is that perhaps you are a little shames-faced about it all, so you keep quiet.

We demand that your Party explain to the international and British working class why you supported, and still support, Stalin's murders of the majority of the Bolshevik Party leadership.

G. Healy,
Secretary, Socialist Labour League.

-oOo-

The Elements of Dialectics

Reference Lenin *Collected Works*, Volume 38 page 221

Having made a thorough conspectus on Hegel's *Science of Logic* from the materialist standpoint Lenin summarised his results into 16 "Elements of Dialectics". These prove to be extraordinarily helpful not only for initial study, but as a means of correctly grasping the change and development of the external world on a daily basis. Gerry Healy often said that if we negate the world into thought materialisticly we negate dialectical logic into thought with it, because movement according to such logic is the mode of existence of matter. It is crucial, however, the proceed materialistically and be conscious of this logic, and it takes practice. If we neglect to practice we shall never grasp dialectical thought and we can lose the skill once having mastered it. That is the meaning of Trotsky's advice:

> "Dialectic training of the mind, as necessary to a revolutionary fighter as finger exercise to a pianist, demands approaching all problems as *processes* and not as *motionless categories*. Whereas vulgar evolutionists, who limit themselves generally to recognising evolution in only certain spheres, content themselves in all other questions with the banalities of 'common sense'" (*In Defence of Marxism*, page 70, New Park Publications)

We list the elements below and give our understanding of each in turn.

First Element: The *objectivity* of consideration (not examples, not divergencies, but the Thing-in-itself)

The thing-in-itself is the object we perceive in the material world external to thought. At first we sense only its outer form which gives rise to a thought image in sensation. We refer to the thing in the external world as the Identity of the source of sensation, and the image in thought as the indeterminate beginning. It is indeterminate because we are conscious only of its outer form while the inner truth or Essence of the thing is still unknown to us, and it is a beginning because if we continue to observe the thing in its movement and life we can discover its inner truth, Essence. In this way we bring this process of cognition to a definite conclusion by establishing the truth or Essence of the thing we perceive, and transform this beginning by bringing it to a definite end. We come to know the Identity of the source of sensation as a *quality*, a definite determinate thing.

This is the Marxist, dialectical materialist way of reflecting the external material world in thought.

It is materialist because we allow the world we experience to immediately determine our consciousness without imposing our own thoughts we already have upon it. We must not, Lenin warns us, try to understand it by comparison with other things which appear similar, (examples), or drift off at a tangent by considering other unconnected things, (divergencies). It is dialectical because the whole process manifests the dialectical laws of all motion, be it material or thought. These laws were first elaborated by G.W.F Hegel in an idealist way: He held that it was thought that determined the world we perceive, and as a result there was some error and confusion in his theory. Later, Karl Marx clarified Hegel's view by grasping that the reverse was the truth and in this way made a science of thought itself. The external world is the cause of all thought and our Ideas reflect it. This is the materialist view. Frederick Engels, Marx's life-long comrade, worked with Marx to perfect their dialectical materialist philosophy, and he set out the laws of dialectical motion as follows:

1. All progress takes place through the unity and conflict, interpenetration and transformation of opposites.

2. The transformation of quality into quantity and from quantity back to quality

3. The law of the negation of the negation.

Lenin studied this theory in great depth and became its master. In Volume 38 of is *Collected Works* we find his conspectus of Hegel's great work, *The Science of Logic*. This logic falls into three parts, *The Doctrine of Being,* the *Doctrine of Essence*, and the *Doctrine of the Notion.* The best starting point is the *Doctrine of Essence* which begins of page 129 in the 1972 printing.

"The truth of Being is Essence ... Being is the immediate. Knowledge seeks to understand that truth which Being, *in and for itself*, is, and therefore it does not halt ... at the immediate and its determinations, but *penetrates* through it, assuming that *behind* this being there is something other than Being itself, and that this background constitutes the truth of Being."

The important thing, however, is that this act of "penetration" consists in observing the thing, (Identity), over a period of *time,* that is, we see it in its *movement and life*, not as a dead, fixed image. This is the crucial difference between Marxist, dialectical cognition, and all forms of idealist, non-dialectical thought. The latter way is to impose thoughts from memory, "Oh, I know what this is ..." This is the idealist method, letting thought determine what is seen, the external world. But the secret of dialectical thought is to understand *time*, and how it passes, because motion though time and space is the *mode of existence of matter and thought*, their very Essence, and that includes the thing-in-itself as we perceive it in sensation and thought. We attempt an explanation.

If we time an event, say with a stopwatch, we click in the present and watch the hand rotate. The first click, the start of the event, is now getting older and older; we say it is "proceeding into the past". At the end of the event we click it again, in a new moment of the present. Thought is the same. Like the click, we start in the present and then observe the passing of time, proceeding into the past, but each time we must return to the present to reconnect our senses with the material world, because only the present exists – the past has gone and the future not yet come. Let us return to Lenin, quoting Hegel:

"This path of knowledge seems to be the 'activity of cognition, external to being … however this movement is the movement of Being itself." (*Ibid.*)

It was not just our thought, but both the beginning and the end of the event itself which is the movement of Being measured in time. Next we see how "the truth of being is Essence".

"Essence … it what it is … by virtue of its own infinite movement of Being" (page 130)

The truth, Essence, of the thing is its mode of life and change, and all change takes place according to the dialectical laws of motion we have given above, although each thing-in-itself is in some way, in some small detail, unique, individual. However, all matter is interconnected in reciprocal cause-effect relation, each thing-in-itself existing as part of the whole world and reflecting all that is connected with as their effect, and at this stage we have taken it on its own, isolated from the rest of the material world of which it is a part. Hence although we know it is connected with other things-in-themselves as effect to their cause, we do not yet know what its true essence is – its Essence is hidden within it – it is "in-itself".

Throughout the Marxist method of cognising the external world, (all 16 elements), Essence becomes determinated in a developing way through the dialectical moments of Semblance, Appearance, and Actuality. We grasp the thing-in-itself in the moment of Semblance.

"These two moments thus constitute Semblance: Nullity, which however persists, and Being, which however is Moment; or again negativity which is in-itself, and reflected immediacy. Consequently these moments are the moments of Essence itself." (page 132)

Being we have explained – it is the reality of the external world in the present moment which we reflect in sensation. Nullity is the non-existence of the past which we experienced by observing the Identity in its movement through time, now in the past, "null", passed away. But yet it *persists* because it is contained in the present moment of Being as its Essence. Grasping this presents insuperable difficulty for the non-Marxist thinker. How can a thing exist yet not exist? "It's a contradiction", they cry. To the Marxist this presents no difficulty because we know that contradiction is the cause of all that exists, and we can resolve each contradiction through dialectical logic, although it takes practice.

In the cognitive moment of Semblance the three laws of the motion of matter and thought are completed. The opposites in unity and conflict are the thing in the external world, the Identity of the source of sensation, and the Image in sensation, the Indeterminate Beginning. As we reflect the Identity in its movement and life through time, both it and the Indeterminate Beginning are opposites in unity and conflict and go through a quantitative process of change. But each changes according to its own nature and not at the same rate, hence the quantitative ratio which unites them changes and reaches a critical value, the moment of Measure at which a qualitative leap takes place and the Indeterminate Beginning becomes determinate as the thing-in-itself in Semblance. But here is the important consideration:

"Thus Semblance is Essence itself, but Essence in a determinateness, and this in such a manner that determinateness is only its moment: Essence is the showing of itself in itself." (Vol 38 page 133)

Essence is the infinite movement of Being, hence Semblance, taken as one finite moment of this movement, as it were frozen it time, is a particular determination of it. But because it is taken at this single moment in time, isolated from all the other things in the external world which are also in motion and which it reflects, it is only a "show" or *manifestation* of Essence. Lenin notes that this single moment of Essence, unconnected with the rest of matter, taken out of its context, is not fully determined:

" ... the unessential, seeming superficial, vanishes more often, does not hold so 'tightly', does not 'sit so firmly' as 'Essence' ... the movement of a river – the foam above and the deep currents below. But even the foam is an expression of essence!" (Page 130. Quotes refer to Hegel)

This "unessential" moment of Essence becomes "essential" through its reconnection in its proper context in the external world. This moment of "foam" is immersed in the river, the external world of which it is a part. This process is expressed in the second element, "the entire totality of the manifold *relations* of this thing to others".

Second element: the entire totality of the manifold *relations* of this thing to others.

When dealing with the first element we said that the thing-in-itself in Semblance contained Essence in an unessential way – it did not "sit firmly", and that this was because we had taken it out of its context in the material world external to thought. The Essence of this thing can only be proved by relating it to all the other things with which it was connected in the external world and which it must reflect. This element must be understood in unity with the third element below.

Third Element: The *development* of the thing (phenomenon, respectively), its own movement, its own life.

Semblance is a moment in our cognitive process, the reflection in thought of the Identity of the source of sensation. If we observe this thing in two successive moments in time and compare its second condition with its first, we can see the difference, how it has changed and developed. We call this "the Difference within the Identity", and it is the way it moves, how it changes that is its truth or Essence. Each moment reflects the other, the present resulting from, reflecting, the past and vice versa, and the past reflecting the present. Essence is "reflection into itself". So now we know exactly how this thing moves, but there is still a further question – Semblance only "shows" us Essence, but why does this thing move *precisely in this way* and no other?

This thing exists in a world of many such things, all moving and changing, and every one is affected by any number of things with which it may be connected in some way. The real cause of its precise motion is the algebraic sum of all these differently acting causes, so we must consider this thing in all its manifold relations to other things.

Development consists in change with additional content and increasing complexity, all the relations, (reflection), between each new content, (opposite). This is the movement and life of the thing-in-itself. The phenomenon is the developing reflection of the thing in sensation and thought.

Fourth Element: the internally contradictory *tendencies* (*and* sides) in this thing.

Example: First opposite - workers in dispute vote to strike. Second opposite - full time organiser refuses to make it official. The result of this contradiction is neither the one nor the other but, say, limited sanctions. This third opposite tends to change this thing in some *new* way, and so on. The more opposites as tendencies that are correctly included the more profoundly true the Essence of the thing-in-itself

Fifth Element: the thing (phenomenon etc.) as the sum *and unity of opposites*.

The sum, obviously, is the totality of the opposite sides and tendencies, (quantity). The unity is their interconnectedness into one whole thing, a quality.

Sixth Element: the struggle, respectively unfolding, of these opposites, contradictory strivings etc.

These opposites do not all come at once but over time, hence the truth, Essence, of the thing progressively unfolds, each opposite contradicting each other, causing change in different directions. Those who have studied mechanics will understand this as being like a diagramme of forces, the summation of the vectors giving the resultant.

Seventh element: The union of analysis and synthesis – the break-down of the separate parts and the totality, the summation of these parts.

We break down the external world into its parts, and gather them into the content of the thing-in itself. Breaking down a whole into its pasts is analysis, and bringing them into the thing-in-itself as one whole is synthesis. Clearly both of these processes are united into a *single* process; analysis and synthesis are two sides of a coin and always come together. The are "self-related opposites", like positive and negative.

Eighth Element: the relations of each thing (phenomenon etc.) are not only manifold, but general, universal. Each thing (phenomenon, process etc.) is connected with *every other*.

Each thing in this unity is related to every other and therefore reflects every other in itself. Lenin explains this comprehensively:

"… the opposites (the individual is opposed to the universal) are identical: the individual exists only in the connection that leads to the universal. The universal exists only in the individual and through the individual. Every individual is (in one way or another) a universal. Every universal is (a fragment, or an aspect, or the Essence of) an individual …" (Vol. 38 page 361)

Any individual thing is one of a kind. *This* individual thing, say a house, is individual because it is unique in some way. But it is universal because it is a concrete case of the abstract concept "house". But this universal contains nothing of the reality, it is only a fragment of the individual, just sufficient to establish the Essence, walls, roof etc.

Ninth Element: not only the unity of opposites, but the *transitions* of **every** determination, quality, feature, side, property into *every* other [into its opposite?]

This element expresses the interrelations of the parts more profoundly, establishing the *Substance* of the whole. The concept of Substance expresses the inner unity of the motion of matter which gives rise to the Form of the whole.

Tenth Element: the endless process of discovery of *new* sides, relations etc.
We now follow the fate of the thing-itself in the present, in its context in the external, changing world. Each day presents new developments and relations with changes and new opposites. It is an infinite process which deepens and enriches man's knowledge of the world.

Eleventh Element: the endless process of the deepening of man's knowledge of the thing, of phenomena, processes etc, from Appearance to Essence and from less profound to more profound Essence.

We are now approaching a more concrete understanding of the thing and the world of which it is a part. The concept of Appearance expresses the moment of cognition where the phenomenon (thought reflection) contains the Essence of the world situation and the thing-itself as a *moving* part of it. However, Essence is not explicitly expressed in Appearance, but only in a hidden way. We can explain this by reference to the old adage of the falling tree: "If a tree falls in a forest and there is no one there to hear it, does it still make a noise?" The trite answer is yes, but this is wrong. The falling tree makes *no* sound – it sets up shock-waves in the air which activate the sense of hearing in men and animals. The sound is Appearance, the shock-waves the Essence.

Twelfth Element: from Existence to Causality and from one form of connection and reciprocal dependence to another, deeper, more general form.

The concept of Existence expresses the thing in its essential connections in the world. That which is not in external connections in the world (abstract Being) does not exist. Causality is the unity of Cause and Effect. Clearly that which is effected by another is at the same time changing it is some way, is a cause upon it, and vice versa. This is reciprocal dependence leading to new forms.

Thirteenth Element: the repetition at a higher stage of certain features, properties etc of the lower and …

Fourteenth Element: … the apparent return to the old (negation of the negation).

These two elements must be understood as manifesting the law of the negation of the negation. The first law, the unity and conflict of opposites, is the struggle of two opposite qualities as a process through time. This is the first (quantitative) negation. In the moment of Measure this first negation is terminated. This is the negation of the (first) negation. These two are transformed through the transformation of quantity into a new quality, but the content of each is carried forward, sublated into the new quality. Each opposite is negated yet preserved in the new quality as its content in altered form. This appears as a return to their previous, original form, but the Essence is transformed

Fifteenth Element: the struggle of content with form and conversely. The throwing off of the form, the transformation of the content.

Content and Form are dialectically related. As new content comes into Being it necessarily takes on its own Form. But this new Form exists in caused/effect relation with other Forms with which it is in unity and conflict and is changed by them. In turn the change of Form alters the content.

Sixteenth Element: the transition of quantity into quality and vice versa. (15 and 16 examples of 9)

We explained this with respect to Element Fourteen.

-oOo-

Letters to a Group

In this section we reproduce a selection of letters submitted for discussion by a group of labour activists.

Our "Marxist" Discussion Group

Any open discussion on Marxist theory is a struggle between this theory, dialectical materialism, and the dominant ideology in our class-divided society, that of the ruling class, the bourgeoisie. Their ideology is subjective idealism based on anti-dialectical logic, metaphysical formalism. This is the class struggle at the subjective, theoretical level. The contradiction between these two ideologies is reflected in every moment of Being, in our group as a whole, and in every individual one of us, and of course the totality of the class struggle as material reality. This is the Essence of the present historical moment and it has, inevitably, been the driving contradiction of our group.

So far the directly theoretical submissions I have tabled in a struggle for Marxist theory are as follows:

Elements of Dialectics
Quantity and Quality
Three Sources and Three Component Parts of Marxism. (Lenin Vol 19, page 23)
Thesis – Marxism is Dialectical Materialism
Materialism Nailed Down
Trotsky's Theory of Permanent Revolution
What is Marxism – What is Not Marxism?
Marxism and Statistics

Apart from some occasional comment in meetings I do not recall ever having had a reply to any of them which was based on this Essential Marxist theory. Substantially the content of the discussion has been confined to narrow political and economic questions treated formally. Even our study of Volume 1 of *Capital*, although valuable, has been treated as formal political economy rather than dialectical logic. (I once did briefly describe the dialectic of the commodity but there was no discussion.)

Generally speaking, the dialectic of what passes for Marxism in the British working class and bourgeois academia can be determined of as follows:

"I have read some writings of Marx, Engels, Lenin and Trotsky and I agree with them", (*Thesis – affirmation*). "That means I must be a Marxist", (*Anti-thesis- first negation, quantity*). "Since I am a Marxist, then anything I say or think must be Marxism"! (*Synthesis- negation of negation*)"

Every one of us is brought up from birth and educated according to bourgeois ideology, in the belief that there is no other ideology, never has been and never will be. We suffer a blizzard of it from the capitalist media every day and this is an infinitely greater influence upon those who grapple with Marxist theory than a few fragments of Marxist literature they have encountered and only superficially understood according to formal, anti-dialectical logic.

This kind of thinking has taken substantial form as a philosophical *genre*, a social form of consciousness the content of which is individuals and various organisations claiming to be Marxist. Disastrously, this social layer is substantially influenced by the universities which teach a sort of *pastiche* of Marxism robbed of its revolutionary Essence, its negative self-relation. Generally such people, in the mistaken belief that the ruling class would train its deadly enemies in its own educational institutions (!), accept such teaching as true Marxism. Proud of their academic achievement, they cling tenaciously to them in the belief that they complement Marxist theory rather than absolutely negate it. But, Lenin informs us, there is no such thing as neutral science in a class divided society. This is the way the ruling class fights Marxism; it cannot refute it so it must propagate a false version and lead the working class to it through the so called "Marxist" organisations and tame professors.

How can we understand our own group in the light of this social context, the class struggle at the level of theory? First, we must understand the group as a whole, a *sum and unity of opposites*, parts, and we must see our own individual selves as parts of this whole – determined by it. *The Elements of Dialects*, (Lenin Vol. 38 page 221), all of them, describe such a unity in its movement, life and development. Along with this development each individual one of us will develop as an individual, but what we learn, and the changes we make, come from our consciousness of the development of the *whole group*.

This was, uniquely, Gerry Healy's method of training. He repeatedly insisted that "we do not have a teacher/pupil relationship." Every member of the group *had* to contribute to the discussion, no matter how inexperienced, because each person was a part of the whole and in some way determined the life and movement of that whole.

Healy would remain silent till he had heard enough to be able to determine the Essence of the whole in the given moment, from which point, because of his mastery of the dialectic, he was able to lead the group forward to grasping deeper, more profound Essence of itself. This, ultimately, is the *only* way Marxist cadres can be trained. Methods which remain at the level of the individual can *never* succeed. If we can succeed in this way we can truly claim to be Marxists as individuals and as a group, and we shall develop revolutionary theory and practice. It is not at all fanciful to say that we could change the course of history. But this is only a beginning. We must, as a historical necessity, go on to build many such groups, train Marxist cadres, and to unite them into a new international leadership for the working class.

There is Still Another Matter.
Reply to a Paper on the Labour Party

We call our group the Marxist Discussion Group, but we do not discus Marxist theory. When we speak of Marxist theory, we mean the same as Lenin did, the dialectical process of cognition originated by Karl Marx. The author of this paper approaches his subject according to this science, but his document is not a discussion of Marxist theory, it is a discussion of the Labour Party. I have had some success in the past in explaining such difference by advancing this analogy.

When I worked in a factory I would go in in the morning, look at the job and pick up a micrometer. The micrometer measures the job, reflects its truth or Essence. The job is object, cause, the micrometer is subject, effect. But there was still another matter. You looked at the wall and there was a coloured plaque. If the coloured tag on the micrometer was the same colour it was OK, but if it wasn't you went to the standards room and exchanged it for one that had the right tag. They had to be re-calibrated every month. That's what *we* must do. We keep studying the job, but a discussion of Marxist theory involves a trip to the standards room to re-calibrate our mental micrometer. Marxist theory is epistemology, a theory of cognition. When we study Marxist theory we are concerned with the micrometer, not the job.

Of course we have political theories, social theories, and historical theories, but these cannot be taken separately from our theory of knowledge because although they are different they are also the same. These particular theories on political questions such as the nature of the Labour Party or economic questions relate to our dialectical materialist theory of knowledge as genus and species. They are all just concretisations of it. So if we don't study and master the general theory of Marxism, our theory of knowledge, none of the particular theories will be right. If we don't calibrate our micrometer we shall scrap the job.

A discussion of Marxist theory is a discussion of our thought process, *how* we think, *not* what we think about, *and certainly not what we know*. But how does that work? What does it mean to think about thought? This seems to make thought one thing and two separate things simultaneously – that's impossible, it's a contradiction, says the formal thinker. But not the dialectical thinker - he knows that everything is itself and the other of itself simultaneously – we say it is "negatively self-related". That which does not contradict itself does not exist.

This is the key to Marxist theory, but it does present some difficulty because although it starts out as a matter of *understanding* an idea, it must become a *practice*. For the Marxist thought is a *practice* – we deliberately do it, don't we? We decide to think about something and then go ahead and do it. What's the difference between that and deciding to dig a ditch and digging it? This is what we mean when we say practice is the highest point of theory, although there is a bit more to that.

So becoming a Marxist is to unite thought and practice in this contradictory way according to the dialectical laws of motion of matter and thought, and those who have not mastered this skill are *not* Marxists, any more than the bloke who can't use a micrometer is a centre-lathe turner. We can't understand the Labour Party as Marxists till we have trained ourselves to do it in the Marxist way. But it takes practice, and if we cease to practice we will lose it, that's why Trotsky speaks of finger exercise for the concert pianist. I have known excellent Marxists in the past who have suddenly become appalling reactionaries because they stopped practicing. The best starting point is Hegel's *Doctrine of Essence* as transformed into the materialist Marxist theory, because it brings the external world, (Being), and thought into unity as opposites in conflict. We find it in Volume 38 of Lenin's Collected Works, page 87 in the 1972 printing. I recently gave a brief explication in reference to the first element of dialectics. Over many years I have explained it again and again. At first my explanations were indeterminate and contained error, but I gradually improved and I think I have got it right now. My latest and best explanation will appear in the second volume of my *Marxist Anthology* shortly, I will circulate a word version at some point. Let us begin a discussion of Marxist theory based on this. I'm not asking anyone to take my word for anything – everything is referenced back to the classics. Study them – or change the name of the group.

Terry Button
14.4.2020

Letter From a Comrade on Marx's Capital

Marx writes about the division of labour in both manufacture and society. He briefly distinguishes manufacture from industry: based on handicraft, manufacture remains labour intensive; large scale industry is machinery dominant. The division of labour in manufacture is merely a particular method of creating relative surplus value at the expense of the worker whose value is reduced and his mental faculties crippled by undemanding, simple and repetitive work. Workers are graded according to their relative value, skilled and unskilled, to the detriment of all. Skilled workers are most prone to resist reduction in their value.

The division of labour in society between manufacturers can only be achieved fully by industry. It is mediated and controlled through the sale and purchase of commodities. Density of population, a combination of population and communication, is important.

25 April 2020

In Reply

In our discussion of Capital we have fallen into the common trap of reading it according to formal logic instead of the dialectical logic upon which it rests, and without which the secret of capitalist production, labour *power* as a commodity producing *surplus value* could not have been laid bare. The formal understanding of the labour theory of value was known to David Ricardo, but it took dialectical logic the explain the production of *surplus value*, and we will understand it no other way.

To discuss any Marxist classic we must start from exactly referenced text and proceed dialectically through analysis and synthesis to new understanding. All I see before me is paraphrasing and some suggested conclusions and clearly it is not possible to generalise to this extent without losing the Essence of the content. (The *whole* of chapter 14 no less!)

One such suggestion, if I have it right, is that the production of relative surplus value reduces the "value of the worker". Nowhere does Marx speak of the value of the worker, but rather the value of his labour power, and this is not determined by his *own* labour, but the labour of others who produce the commodities he needs to live and work.

We need to be clear as to the concept of relative surplus value. *All social* labour under *any* system is based on a division of labour, not just manufacture or machine industry. I take it that what is being suggested is that a *change* in the division of labour changes the level of relative surplus value, but firstly the intention of the capitalist is to reduce the *total* labour time and this reduces the value of the commodity. The capitalist gains by driving competitors out of the market.

No doubt the rate of relative surplus value would also be changed, but this must be determined in relation to the rate of *necessary* surplus value which fluctuates. Relative surplus value is the additional value expropriated by the capitalist by increasing the ratio of surplus value to the necessary value during the same work period. That's why it's called "relative". It is explained on page 312

I think that at this point we should begin our study of Capital again from the beginning and struggle to understand in according to the dialectical logic upon which it is based. No doubt there are still questions left unanswered but I am busy at the moment with the second volume of my Anthology. I will return to this.

Terry Button
April 2020

-oOo-

Marxism and Statistics

The examination of an economic or social system by statistical methods is profoundly materialistic. In order to arrive at a true reflection of the movement and life of the global capitalist system, and to grasp the truth of any finite moment in its movement, at least a minimum of general statistical analysis is necessary. Socialist planning would be completely impossible without having statistical experts at the disposal of every government department.

Towards the end of the nineteenth century Lenin carried out the most detailed statistical work, particularly with respect to the feudal economic system. In 1893 he studied the work of Postnikov, a bourgeois economist, who revealed that an average family of 6 needed to have 18 desssiatines under crops and 3 horses to maintain life. Those who had less had to sell their labour power for wages to survive. Lenin concluded from this that the commodity market was growing and the transition from feudalism to capitalism was taking place. (Lenin Collected Works Vol. 1 page 52. One dessiatine is equal to 1.09 hectares.)

This seems to be common sense, but what is the *dialectical* reasoning for Lenin's conclusion? As we approach, (statistically), the smaller farms the income from farming quantitatively reduces as compared with that possible from wage labour. At the critical ratio in the moment of Measure the qualitative transformation takes place, the petty bourgeois farmer, who works his own means of production, (owned or rented makes no difference to this consideration), becomes a proletarian. Lenin further discovers from Postnikov's statistics that 40% of the population had only 10 dessiatines, so there was a drift from feudal agriculture to wage labour, and when the ratio of petty bourgeois to wage labour reaches the moment of Measure feudal farming is transformed into capitalist farming. This is the Marxist way – as opposed to taking it at the level of common sense which *does not make us Marxists just because we agree with Lenin*. It is the *method* which is Marxism, *not* necessarily the conclusion. It's the same conclusion, but not a Marxist conclusion if it is the result of common sense.

If we engage in statistical analysis we must be aware of its limitation or we shall fall into fatal error. Mathematics is the science of magnitude, quantity, and we can never arrive at such understanding as did Lenin if we do not understand this limitation. Mathematics is limited to consideration of *quantity* and it can never make the transition to *quality* and relate the two. Lenin's conclusion above does this – the reduction of income to below subsistence level gives rise to the *qualitative leap* from petty bourgeois production to proletarian wage labour. Only dialectical logic could have brought this to consciousness. Certainly Postnikov did not get it, nor did he get Lenin's further generalisation that the summation of these individual cases approached the qualitative leap from feudal to capitalist economy.

Here is another case from history. In 1914 the workers movement in Russia was divided into a legal struggle, mostly Mensheviks, and an illegal struggle, the Marxist revolutionary struggle, the Bolsheviks led by Lenin with the newspaper *Pravda*. The legal organisations considered that a reformist struggle was the right way and called for the illegal party be liquidated. In order to compare the support each side received from the workers Lenin collected statistics to show the level of support their respective newspapers received. He studied the figures from 1 January to 13 May 1914 for St. Petersburg, Moscow and the provinces and discovered the following:

	Number of Collections	Sum Collected
Pravdist	3586	Rb 21584
Liquidationist	1124	Rb 12056

We conclude that quantitatively the Pravdists have most support, but what of the quality? To find this Lenin placed the sum and the number collected in each case in unity in the moment of Measure and made the qualitative leap.

$$\text{Liquidtionist} \quad 12056/1124 = 11$$
$$\text{Pravdist} \quad 21584/3586 = 6$$

So the *size* of donations received by the liquidationists was nearly twice that of the Pravdists, indicating the *quality* of their support; it came from workers with higher incomes, the "working class aristocracy" etc, while the quality of the Pravdists support was mainly the lower paid proletariat of more revolutionary outlook. (Taken from *The Working Class and its Press*, Collected Works Volume 20. Page 364)

This is a simple example, but it shows that the relation of quality to quantity cannot be expressed by statistics – it takes a dialectically trained mind to logically transcend the limitation of mathematical expression. Marxism begins where statistics end. Statistics are generally used to express the change in a given parameter over time, such as Gross National Product. In this case the two quantities in unity in the moment of Measure are the levels of GNP separated by a time interval, but once again the truth of such a comparison can only be grasped by dialectical logic.

One statistical fact does not tell us the truth of the moment it reflects, its negative self-relation, nor does a string of statistical facts express the dialectical relation between them, the law governed nature of the process they represent. We can explain this best by referring to Trotsky's explanation of the dialectic:

"I will here attempt to sketch the substance of the problem in a very concise form. The Aristotelian logic of the simple syllogism starts from the proposition that 'A' is equal to 'A'. This simple postulate is accepted as an axiom for a multitude of practical human actions and elementary generalisations. But in reality 'A' is never equal to 'A'. This is easy to prove if we observe these two letters under a lens – they are quite different from each other. But, one can object, the question is not the size or the form of the letters, since they are only symbols for equal quantities, for instance a pound of sugar. The objection is beside to point; in reality a pound of sugar is never equal to a pound of sugar – a more delicate scale always discloses a difference. Again one can object: but a pound of sugar is equal to itself. Neither is this true – all bodies change uninterruptedly in size, weight, colour, etc. They are never equal to themselves. A sophist will respond that a pound of sugar is equal to itself 'at any given moment.' Aside from the extremely dubious practical value of the 'axiom', it does not withstand theoretical criticism either. How should we really conceive the word 'moment'? If it is an infinitesimal interval of time, then a pound of sugar is subjected during the course of this 'moment' to inevitable changes. Or is the 'moment' a purely mathematical abstraction, that is, a zero of time? But everything exists in time; and existence itself is an uninterrupted process of transformation; time is consequently a fundamental element of existence. Thus the axiom 'A' is equal to 'A' signifies that a thing is equal to itself if it does not change, that is, if it does not exist.

"At first glance it could seem that these 'subtleties' are useless. In reality they are of decisive significance. The axiom the 'A' is equal to 'A' appears on the one hand to be the point of departure for all our knowledge, on the other hand the point of departure for all the errors in our knowledge. To make use of the axiom 'A' is equal to 'A' with impunity is possible only within certain limits. When quantitative changes in 'A' are negligible for the task at hand then we can assume that 'A' is equal to 'A'. That is, for example, the manner in which a buyer and a sell consider a pound of sugar … But quantitative changes beyond certain limits become converted to qualitative. A pound of sugar subjected to the action of water or kerosene ceases to be a pound of sugar … To determine at the right moment the critical point where quantity changes to quality is one of the most important and difficult tasks in all the spheres of knowledge including sociology," (*In Defence of Marxism*, New Park Publications, page 63.)

This is an excellent explanation of dialectical motion. It has been necessary to quote at such length to show how we must understand statistical content and exposition, because it all depends on whether we allow the axiom 'A' is equal to 'A' to be the point of departure for all our knowledge or the point of departure for all the errors in our knowledge. If we fail to transcend the limits of statistical analysis we shall suffer repeated error as to the truth, Essence, of the process we have in view.

-oOo-

Hegel's Remarks on the Doctrine of Essence

Hegel begins his explication of the *Doctrine of Essence* with a chapter titled *Illusory Being (Schein). Schein* is German for "show", and it gives us the idea of what he means by illusory being; a false, limited, superficial, fleeting presentation of the material world to the senses. He gives the moments of the theory of *Illusory Being* as follows:

"Essence that issues from Being seems to confront it as an opposite; this immediate being is, in the first instance, the unessential

"But secondly, it is more than unessential being, it is essenceless being, it is illusory being.

"Thirdly, this illusory being is not something external to or other than essence; on the contrary, it is essence's own illusory being. The showing of this illusory being within essence itself is reflection." (*Science of Logic,* Humanity Books, page 394)

On page 133 in Volume 38 of his Collected Works, in his conspectus on Hegel's *Science of Logic,* Lenin, working from a different translation, uses the term *Semblance* instead of *Show* or *Illusory being*. It is the same thing. He makes these three notes:

"Thus Semblance is Essence itself, but Essence in a determinateness, and this in such a manner that determinateness is only its moment: Essence is the showing of itself in itself." (Lenin quoting Hegel)

"That which shows itself is essence in *one* of its determinations, in one of its aspects, in one of its moments. *Essence* seems to be just that. Semblance is the showing (Scheinen) of essence itself in itself." (Lenin's note)

"Essence contains Semblance within itself, as infinite internal movement ..." ... "In this its self-movement Essence is reflection. Semblance is the same as Reflection." (Lenin quoting Hegel)

So this show of the material world, in a moment of human cognition we call Semblance, is actually a show of the Essence, or truth. But it is only one moment of the eternal movement of that world, like one frame of the reel of a moving film showing the world in its motion. And this one moment is the same as reflection. But reflection contains *two* things or moments, the reflection and that which is reflected. This is a contradiction - how can two moments be contained in one? To understand the concept of Reflection we must first consider the philosophical concept of Contradiction.

The *Science of Logic* is one long exposition of the logic of human cognition of the world external to thought. Hegel, we know, was an objective idealist, he believed that only thought existed and that the world we perceive through our senses was thought itself in some objective form. Consequently, he constructed his world of logic from thought itself, a monumental and contradictory process some of which, it turned out, had no basis in reality and contained error. However, the core of his logic was sound, a work of brilliant genius and of historical importance, and really did reflect the material world. Hegel frequently interrupts the flow of his brilliant logical exposition with *"Remarks"*, supplementary explanation of the logical process. Sometimes there are two or three at once and can be several pages long, and give good clarification of the logic. We find a Remark on the concept of

Reflection on page 404, and another Remark on the concept of Contradiction on page 439. Since Contradiction is the most fundamental of *all* concepts we shall deal with this *Remark* first.

Remark 3: The Law of Contradiction

"If, now, the first determination of reflection, namely, identity, difference and opposition, have been put in the form of a law, still more should the determination into which they pass as their truth, namely, contradiction, be grasped and enunciated as a law: *everything is inherently contradictory,* and in the sense that this law in contrast to the others expresses rather the truth and the essential nature of such things. The contradiction that makes its appearance in opposition, is only the developed nothing that is contained in identity and that appears in the expression that the law of identity says *nothing.* This negation further determines itself into difference and opposition, which now is the posited contradiction."

Formal, "normal", thinking takes everything as a simple identity of some kind, "this is a ...", whatever it is. The law of Identity says this thing is itself and cannot be another thing simultaneously. A equals A, A cannot equal not-A. But it is clear that this says nothing at all about A, the statement is dead and meaningless. In reality A is changing all the time, everything comes into being and passes away in time. This means that if we observe A in two successive moments then A in the second moment is different to A at the first, contradicts the first and can be opposed to it as different; the "nothing", no difference, as expressed as A = A, has developed into opposition of the two moments, the second moment contradicts the first. "A is *not* the same. A is *different*" to A. Hegel continues:

"But it is one of the fundamental prejudices of logic as hitherto understood and of ordinary thinking, that contradiction is not so characteristically essential and immanent a determination as identity; but, in fact, if it were a question of grading the two determinations and they had to be kept separate, then contradiction would have to be taken as the profounder determination and more characteristic of essence. For as against contradiction, identity is merely the determination of the simple immediate, of dead being; but contradiction is the root of all movement and vitality; it is only in so far as something has a contradiction within it that it moves, had an urge and activity.

"In the first place, contradiction is usually kept aloof from things, from the sphere of being and of truth generally; it is asserted that there is *nothing that is contradictory*. Secondly, it is shifted into subjective reflection by which it is first posited in the process of relating and comparing. But even in this reflection, it does not really exist, for it is said that the *contradictory* cannot be *imagined* or *thought*. Whether it occurs in actual things of in reflective thinking, it ranks in general as a contingency, a kind of abnormality and a passing paroxysm of sickness."

Here Hegel, the idealist, surrenders to materialism. Contradiction is inherent in all things, all Identities in the physical real world and is the source of all movement ad life, and since movement pre-supposes the passing of time, and everything exists in time, then if a thing does not move it does not exist. Contradiction, then, is the most fundamental cause of all Being, and it is a far more true and important concept than Identity. But, Hegel points out, ordinary thinking, that is the kind of thinking normal for bourgeois society and upon which all our knowledge is based, does not comprehend contradiction, and where the material world presents contradiction to the formal thinker he considers that a mistake is being made and ignores it. This kind of thinking informs all aspects of modern society, even well known philosophers and scientists, and is a huge barrier to human progress. We are all taught to think this way from birth. Hegel again:

"Now as regards the assertion that *there is* no contradiction, that it does not exist, this statement need not cause us any concern; an absolute determination of essence must be present in every experience, in every actual, as in every notion. We made the same remark above in connexion with the infinite, which is the contradiction as displayed in the sphere of being. But common experience itself enunciates it when it says that at least *there is* a *host* of contradictory things, contradictory arrangements, whose contradiction exists not merely in an external reflection but in themselves. Further, it is not to be taken merely as an abnormality which only occurs here and there, but is rather the negative as determined in the sphere of essence, the principle of all self-movement, which consists solely in an exhibition of it. External, sensuous motion itself is contradiction's immediate existence. Something moves, not because at one moment it is here and at another there, but at one and the same moment it is here and not here, because in this 'here', it at once is and is not. The ancient dialecticians must be granted the contradictions that they pointed out in motion; but it does not follow that therefore there is no motion, but on the contrary, that motion is existent contradiction itself."

This *"host* of contradictory things, contradictory arrangements, whose contradiction exists not merely in an external reflection but in themselves", contain their own identifying Essence because they all move and change in their own way; their movement is not only observable in external appearances, but is internal and contained withing them – the *are* moving. The Contradiction of motion consists in the fact that a thing must be in two places at once, because if it rests in one place it has ceased to move. It is the negative because motion continually negates immediate Being, renders it past, null. This is now established as a physical fact by modern science in the form of Heisenberg's "uncertainty principle".

As a thing moves it changes. In its first moment we take it as Positive Identity, but it its second moment it is different, is the Negative of the first, "not the first". We call this change the Difference within the Identity. The difference between them is *Contradiction.* We shall not follow Hegel's note on contradiction further, but now consider his note on the concept of Reflection.

"Remark.

"Reflection is usually taken in a subjective sense as the movement of the faculty of judgement that goes beyond the given immediate conception and seeks universal determination for it or compares such determinations with it. Kant opposes *reflective judgement* to *determining judgment.* He defines the faculty of judgement in general as the ability to *think the particular as subsumed under the universal. If the universal is given* (the rule, principle, law), then the faculty of judgement that subsumes the particular under it is *determinative.* But if only the particular is given *for which the universal is to be found,* then judgement is merely *reflective*. Here, then, to reflect is likewise to go beyond an immediate to the universal."

It is important to grasp what is being said here since we must think logically, and be conscious of our logical processes as we proceed. We are familiar with the term reflection in this sense. The immediate is the thing we sensuously perceive before we begin to think about it. We begin to think about it but we are not always conscious of how thought proceeds through forms of motions, patterns and structures. We see an individual house and immediately know what it is, because we know what houses *are*. The house is the individual, houses as such are the universal. The individual *reflects* the universal. This is reflection as it occurs in thought - thoughts connected up in this way show the truth of what we see or experience. Kant's determinating judgement is simply the act of deciding what a thing is ... we judge the thing we see to be a house - we *determine* the thing as a house and not some other thing. Reflective judgement shows that the individual thing is connected with this universal which may tell us something about it but nothing more. So our thoughts reflect each other, are connected with each other in definite ways and change and develop according to the laws of logic. As class fighters we must master such logical thought in order to grasp the truth of our class struggle and adopt the correct practice. Hegel goes on:

> "On the one hand, it is only through this reference of the immediate to its universal that it is determined as particular; by itself, in it only an individual or an immediate, simply affirmative being. On the other hand, that to which it is referred is its universal, its rule, principle, law, in general, that which is reflected into itself, is self-related, essence or the essential."

When we refer this *individual* thing, *this* house, to the universal, abstract concept, house, we know it only as one of many houses, a *particular* kind of thing, a "simply affirmative being". But the universal is its rule, principle, law, it is reflected in the thing as its own *inner truth,* not in its stillness and death, but as its law it determines the form of its life and *motion* through time. Its outward reflection determines its self-related essence, or its "reflection-into-self". Referring back to the quotes from Lenin we gave above, we find this:

> "Semblance (that which shows itself) is the *Reflection* of Essence in (it) itself." (Vol. 38 page 133)

We can visualise two successive moments in the motion (Becoming) of a thing as mirrors facing inwards to each other. The first is Identity, and the second is reflected Difference. Each mirror reflects the other "in itself" But since each is a reflecting mirror, then reflection is reflected in reflection, Essence as reflection-into-self. If we reduce the differential to a finite moment of time containing the infinite there is still a potential for difference to unfold and this is *Contradiction*, the source of all Being, all movement and life.

-oOo-

Trade Unions in the Epoch of Imperialist Decay

By

L. Trotsky

Foreword

With the return of the Blairites to full control of the Labour Party following the Election of Sir Keir Starmer to the leadership in May 2020, the reaction to the Corbyn leadership is complete. The latter, of course, with its "for the many not the few" socialistic manifesto, is now contained in the history of the Party and will in some measure affect its future. Does this mean that a split is possible?

The Labour Party was created by the working class as an extension of the trade union organisations, and neither the left nor the right of the Labour Party can exist without their financial and organisational support. A split would therefore entail a fight for union support, but the trade unions are in the iron grip of the capitalist state, a grip which was established, and is exercised, by the very Parliamentary system through which both left and right of the Party wish to exercise political power. The depth of opportunism in the traitorous trade union leadership is such that they are bound, by whatever lies and underhand means they find expedient, to support the reaction and leave the left to wither on the vine.

Without doubt the union members will struggle to democratise their organisations, but they can never succeed while in the grip of the capitalist state. This struggle must of course be continued in the most determined manner, but, as Trotsky shows in this article, it can only be done in conjunction with the political struggle external to the unions and the Labour Party, the struggle to build revolutionary organisation under Marxist leadership which, at the same time, will decide the ultimate fate of the Labour Party which rests upon them. (TB)

(The manuscript of the following article was found it Trotsky's desk. Obviously, it was by no means a complete article, but rather the rough notes for an article on the subject indicated by the title. He had been writing them shortly before his death. The Editors.)

Trotsky writes:

There is one common feature in the development, or more correctly the degeneration, of modern trade union organisations in the entire world: it is their drawing closely to and growing together with the state power. This process is equally characteristic in the neutral, the Social-Democratic, the Communist and "anarchist" trade unions. This fact alone shows that the tendency towards "growing together" is intrinsic not in this or that doctrine as such but derives from social conditions common the all unions.

Monopoly capitalism does not rest on competition and free private initiative but on centralised command. The capitalist cliques at the head of mighty trusts, syndicates, banking consortiums, *etcetera*, view economic life from the very same heights as does state power; and they require at every step the collaboration of the latter. In their turn the trade unions in the most important branches of industry find themselves deprived of the possibility of profiting by the competition between the different enterprises. They have to confront a centralized capitalist adversary, intimately bound up with state power.

Hence flows the need of the trade unions – insofar as they remain on reformist positions, *i.e.*, on positions of adapting themselves to private property, to adapt themselves to the capitalist state and to contend for its co-operation. In the eyes of the bureaucracy of the trade union movement the chief task lies in "freeing" the same state from the embrace of capitalism, in weakening its dependence on trusts, in pulling it over to their side. This position is in complete harmony with the social position of the labour aristocracy and the labour bureaucracy, who fight for a crumb in the share of super-profits of imperialist capitalism. The labour bureaucrats do their level best in words and deeds to demonstrate to the "democratic" state how reliable and indispensable they are in peace-time and especially in time of war. By transforming the trade unions into organs of the state, fascism invents nothing new; it merely draws to their ultimate conclusion the tendencies inherent in imperialism.

Colonial and semi-colonial countries are under the sway not of domestic capitalism but of foreign imperialism. However, this does not weaken but on the contrary strengthens the need of direct, daily, practical ties between the magnates of capitalism and the governments which are in essence subject to them – the governments of colonial or semi-colonial countries. Inasmuch as imperialist capitalism creates both in colonies and semi-colonies a stratum of labour aristocracy and bureaucracy, the latter requires the support of colonial and semi-colonial governments, as protectors, patrons and, sometimes, arbitrators. This constitutes the most important social basis for the Bonapartist and semi-Bonapartist character of governments in the colonies and in backward countries generally. This likewise constitutes the basis for the dependence of reformist unions upon the state.

In Mexico the trade unions have been transformed by law into semi-state institutions and have, in the nature of things, assumed a semi-totalitarian character. The statisation of trade unions was, according to the conception of the legislators, introduced in the interests of the workers in order to assure them an influence upon the governmental and economic life. But insofar as foreign imperialist capitalism dominates the national state and insofar as it is able, with the assistance of internal reactionary forces, to overthrow the unstable democracy and replace it with outright fascist dictatorship, to that extent the legislation relating to the trade unions can easily become a weapon in the hands of imperialist dictatorship.

Slogans for Freeing the Unions

From the foregoing it seems, at first sight, easy to draw the conclusion that the trade unions cease to be trade unions in the imperialist epoch. They leave almost no room at all for workers' democracy which, in the good old days, when free trade ruled on the economic arena, constituted the content of the inner life of labour organisations. In the absence of workers' democracy there cannot be any free struggle for the influence over the trade union membership. And because of this, the chief arena of work for revolutionists withing the trade unions disappears. Such a position, however, would be false to the core. We cannot select the arena and the conditions for our activity to suit our own likes and dislikes. It is infinitely more difficult to fight in a totalitarian or a semi-totalitarian state for influence over the working masses than in democracy. The very same thing likewise applies to trade unions whose fate reflects the change in the destiny of capitalist states. We cannot renounce the struggle for influence over workers in Germany merely because the totalitarian regime makes work extremely difficult there. We cannot, precisely in the same way, renounce the struggle within the compulsory labour organisations created by fascism. All the less can we renounce internal systematic work in trade unions of totalitarian and semi-totalitarian type merely because they depend directly or indirectly on the workers state or because the bureaucracy deprived the revolutionists of the possibility of working freely within these trade unions. It is necessary to conduct a struggle under all those concrete conditions which have been created by the preceding developments, including therein the mistakes of the working class and the crimes of its leaders. In the fascist and semi-fascist countries it is impossible to carry on revolutionary work that is not underground, illegal, conspiratorial. Within the totalitarian and semi-totalitarian unions it is impossible or well-neigh impossible to carry on any except conspiratorial work. It is necessary to adapt ourselves to the concrete conditions existing in the trade unions of every given country in order to mobilise the masses, not only against the bourgeoisie, but also against the totalitarian regime within the trade unions themselves and against the leaders enforcing the regime. The primary slogan for this struggle is: *complete and unconditional independence of the trade unions in relation to the capitalist state.* This means a struggle to turn the trade unions into the organs of the broad exploited masses and not the organs of the labour aristocracy.

*   *   *

The second slogan is: *trade union democracy.* This second slogan flows directly from the first and presupposes for its realisation the complete freedom of the trade unions from the imperialist or colonial state.

In other words, the trade unions in the present epoch cannot simply be the organs of democracy as they were in the epoch of free capitalism and they cannot any longer remain politically neutral, that is, limit themselves to serving the daily needs of the working class. They cannot any longer be anarchistic, *i.e.,* ignore the decisive influence of the state on the life of peoples and classes. They can no longer be reformist, because the objective conditions leave no room for any serious and lasting reforms. The trade unions of our time can either serve as secondary instruments of imperialist capitalism for the subordination and disciplining of workers and for obstructing the revolution, or, on the contrary, the trade unions can become the instruments of the revolutionary movement of the proletariat.

The neutrality of trade unions is completely and irretrievably a thing of the past, gone together with the free bourgeois democracy.

*　　　*　　　*

From what has been said it follows quite clearly that, in spite of the progressive degeneration of trade unions and their growing together with the imperialist state, the work within the trade unions not only does not lose any of its importance but remains as before and becomes in a certain sense even more important work than ever for every revolutionary party. The matter at issue is essentially the struggle for influence over the working class. Every organisation, every party, every faction which permits itself an ultimatistic position in relation to the trade unions, *i.e.*, in essence turns its back upon the working class, merely because of displeasure with its organisation, every such organisation is destined to perish. And it must be said it deserves to perish.

*　　　*　　　*

Inasmuch as the chief role in backward countries is not played by national but foreign capitalism, the national bourgeoisie occupies, in the sense of its social position, a much more minor position than corresponds with the development of industry.

Inasmuch as foreign capital does not import workers but proletarianizes the native population, the national proletariat soon begins to play the most important role in the life of the country. In these conditions the national government, to the extent that it tries to show resistance to foreign capital, is compelled to a greater or lesser degree to lean on the proletariat. On the other hand, the governments of those backward countries which consider it inescapable or more profitable for themselves to march shoulder to shoulder with foreign capital, destroy the labour organisations and institute a more or less totalitarian regime. Thus, the feebleness of the national bourgeoisie, the absence of traditions of municipal self-government, the pressure of foreign capitalism and the relatively rapid growth of the proletariat, cut the ground from under any kind of stable democratic regime. The governments of backward, *i.e.,* colonial and semi-colonial countries, by and large assume a Bonapartist or semi-Bonapartist character; and differ in one another in this, that some try to orient in a democratic direction, seeking support among workers and peasants, while others install a form close to military-police dictatorship. This likewise determines the fate of the trade unions. They either stand under the special patronage of the state or they are subjected to cruel persecution. Patronage on the part of the state is dictated by two tasks which confront it: first, to draw the working class closer thus gaining support for resistance against excessive pretensions on the part of imperialism; and, at the same time, to discipline the workers themselves by placing them under the control of a bureaucracy.

*   *   *

Monopoly Capitalism and the Unions

Monopoly capitalism is less and less willing to reconcile itself to the independence of trade unions. It demands of the reformist bureaucracy and the labour aristocracy who pick the crumbs from its banquet table, that they become transformed into a political police before the eyes of the working class. If that is not achieved, the labour bureaucracy is driven away and replaced by the fascists, Incidentally, all the efforts of the labour aristocracy in the service of imperialism cannot in the long run save them from destruction.

The intensification of class contradictions within each country, the intensification of antagonisms between one country and another, produce a situation in which imperialist capitalism can tolerate (i.e., up to a certain time) a reformist bureaucracy only if the latter serves directly as a petty but active stockholder of its imperialist enterprises, of its plans and programmes within the country as well as on the world arena. Social reformism must become transformed into social imperialism in order to prolong its existence, but only prolong it, and nothing more. Because along this road there is no way out in general.

Does this mean that in the epoch of imperialism independent trade unions are generally impossible? It would be fundamentally incorrect to pose the question in this way. Impossible are the independent or semi-independent reformist trade unions. Wholly possible are revolutionary trade unions which not only are not stock-holders of imperialist policy but which set as their task the direct overthrow of the rule of capitalism. In the epoch of imperialist decay the trade unions can be really independent only to the extent that they are conscious of being, in action, the organs of proletarian revolution. In this sense, the programme of transitional demands adopted at the last congress of the Fourth International is not only the programme for the activity of the party but in its fundamental features it is the programme for the activity of the trade unions.

(Translator's note: At this point Trotsky left room on the page to expound further the connection between trade union activity and the Transitional Programme of the Fourth International. It is obvious that implied here is a very powerful argument in favour of military training under trade union control. The following is implied: either the trade unions serve as the obedient recruiting sergeants for the imperialist army and imperialist war or they train workers for self-defence and revolution.)

The development of backward countries is characterised by its combined character. In other words, the last word in imperialist technology, economics, and politics is combined in these countries with traditional backwardness and primitiveness. This law can be observed in the most diverse spheres of the development of colonial and semi-colonial countries, including the sphere of the trade union movement. Imperialist capitalism operates here in its most cynical and naked form. It transports to virgin soil the most perfected methods of its tyrannical rule.

In the trade union movement throughout the world there is to be observed in the last period a swing to the right and the suppression of internal democracy. In England, the Minority Movement in the trade unions has been crushed (not without the assistance of Moscow); the leaders of the trade union movement are today, especially in the field of foreign policy, the obedient agents of the Conservative party. In France there was no room for an independent existence for Stalinist trade unions; they united with the so-called anarcho-syndicalist trade unions under the leadership of Jouhaux and as a result of this unification there was a general shift of the trade union movement not to the left but to the right. The leadership of the

C.G.T. is the most direct and open agency of French imperialist capitalism.

In the United States the trade union movement has passed through the most stormy history in recent years. The rise of the CIO is incontrovertible evidence of the revolutionary tendencies within the working masses. Indicative and noteworthy in the highest degree, however, is the fact that the new "leftist" trade union organisation was no sooner founded than it fell into the steel embrace of the imperialist state. The struggle among the tops between the old federation and the new is reducible in large measure to the struggle for the sympathy and support of Roosevelt and his cabinet.

No less graphic, although in a different sense, is the picture of the development or the degeneration of the trade unions in Spain. In the socialist trade unions all those leading elements which to any degree represented the independence of the trade union movement were pushed out. As regards the anarcho-syndicalist unions, they were transformed into the instrument of the bourgeois republicans; the anarcho-syndicalist leaders became conservative bourgeois ministers. The fact that this metamorphosis took place in conditions of civil war does not weaken its significance. War is the continuation of the self-same policies. It speeds up processes, eposes their basic features, destroys all that is rotten, false, equivocal and lays bare all that is essential. The shift of the trade unions to the right was due to the sharpening of the class and international contradictions. The leaders of the trade union movement sensed or understood, or were given to understand, that now was no time to play the game of opposition. Every oppositional movement within the trade union movement, especially among the tops, threatens to provoke a stormy movement of the masses and create difficulties for national imperialism. Hence flows the swing of the trade unions to the right, and the suppression of workers' democracy within the unions. The basic feature, the swing towards the totalitarian regime, passes through the labour movement of the whole world.

We should also recall Holland, where the reformist and trade union movement was not only a reliable prop of imperialist capitalism, but where the so-called anarcho-syndicalist organisation also was under the control on the imperialist government. The secretary of this organisation, Sneevliet, in spite of his platonic sympathies for the Fourth International was as deputy in the Dutch Parliament most concerned lest the wrath of the government descend upon his trade union organisation.

In the United States the Department of Labour with its leftist bureaucracy has as its task the subordination of the trade union movement to the democratic state and it must be said that this task has up to now been solved with the same success.

The nationalisation of the railways and oilfields in Mexico has of course nothing in common with socialism. It is a measure of state capitalism in a backward country which in this way seeks to defend itself on the one hand against foreign imperialism and on the other against its own proletariat.

The management of railways, oil fields, etc., through labour organisations has nothing in common with workers' control over industry, for in the essence of the matter the management is effected through the labour bureaucracy which is independent of the workers, but in return, completely dependent on the bourgeois state. This measure on the part of the ruling class pursues the aim of disciplining the working class, making it more industrious in the service of the common interests of the state, which appear on the surface to merge with the interests of the working class itself. As a matter of fact, the whole task of the bourgeoisie consists in liquidating the trade unions as organs of the class struggle and substituting in their place the trade union bureaucracy as the organ of the leadership over the workers by the bourgeois state. In these conditions, the task of the revolutionary vanguard is to conduct a struggle for the complete independence of the trade unions and for the introduction of actual workers control over the present union bureaucracy, which has been turned into the administration of railways, oil enterprises and so on.

*   *   *

Events of the last period (before the War) have revealed with especial clarity that anarchism, which in point of theory is always only liberalism drawn to its extremes, was, in practice, peaceful propaganda within the democratic republic, the protection of which it required. If we leave aside individual terrorist act, etc., anarchism, as a system of mass movement and politics, presented only propaganda material under the peaceful protection of the laws. In conditions of crises the anarchists did the opposite of what they taught in peace times. This was pointed out by Marx himself in connection with the Paris Commune. And it was repeated on a far more colossal scale in the experience of the Spanish revolution.

Democratic unions in the old sense of the term, bodies where in the framework of one and the same mass organisation different tendencies struggled more of less freely, can no longer exist. Just as it is impossible to bring back the bourgeois-democratic state, so it is impossible to bring back the old workers' democracy. The fate of one reflects the fate of the other. As a matter of fact, the independence of trade unions in the class sense, in their relations to the bourgeois state, can, in the present conditions, be assured only by a completely revolutionary leadership, that is, the leadership of the Fourth International. This leadership, naturally, must and can be rational and assure the unions the maximum of democracy conceivable under present concrete conditions. But without the political leadership of the Fourth International the independence of the trade unions is impossible.

(The manuscript breaks off here – TB. Taken from *Marxism and the Trade Unions* by L. Trotsky, New Park Publications, 1972)